Praise for What I Learned *f*

"Ron Pappalardo's heart-rending story begins with tragedy but ends with hope and an uplifting message. After losing his son to suicide, the author embarked upon a journey that led to healing and reconciliation—not just for himself, but for his son as well. Along the way, he entered into the realm of the psychic mediums. His writing style reveals the inner workings of this world in a way that is intriguing yet easy to understand.

"What I Learned *from the* Dead is a must-read for anyone who is grieving the loss of a loved one or would like insight into the 'hows' and 'whys' of spirit communication. This book adds weight to our understanding of life after death, life's purpose, and the importance of establishing communication between the two worlds."

Sherrie Dillard, Best-Selling Author,
I'm Still with You and nine other books, and Psychic Medium

"Ron Pappalardo's latest book What I Learned *from the* Dead brings great insight to the world of mediums and those with the gift of communicating with entities on the other side, which includes Ron's own son, who died from suicide. It is a page-turning, read-to-the-finish book that will leave very little doubt about the dynamic state of eternal life that exists after we leave this physical world at death and begin a new life in the spiritual world. A popular guest speaker in my World Religion classes, Ron's book is recommended for people of all religious faiths—and none—who have lost loved ones and wonder about what their life is like on the other side."

Charles S. Chesnavage, PhD
Mercy College, Adjunct Professor of World Religions

"This is a deeply touching story of love between a teenage suicide and his parents. Out of their serious concern about how their son is in the spirit world, their journey to study the other world starts. Their initial experiences of reunion as parents and son through mediums are dramatic and moving because they reveal how strong their mutual love is, in spite of, or even because of, their initial regrets: the parents' regret that they may not have been good enough parents for the son, given his unfortunate incident, and the son's regret that it may have caused his parents much pain.

"Life after death has been an increasingly important topic in Christian theology in recent decades. It is theologically interesting that Pappalardo's book shows, out of his own experiences as a medium, that spirits in the other world, including his son, Joshua, can grow through their relationship of love, not only with earthly people close to them but also with other spirits in the spirit world. It is also noteworthy that he describes God as not only masculine, but feminine as well. One important lesson we can learn from the book is that our mutual love as human beings on Earth, reflecting God's love, is the best preparation for our future transition to the other world. I highly recommend this book."

Theodore Shimmyo, PhD
Unification Theological Seminary, Professor Emeritus of Theology

WHAT I LEARNED
from the DEAD

WHAT I LEARNED
from the DEAD

A Psychic Medium Survives
His Son's Suicide through Spiritualism

Ron Pappalardo

What I Learned *from the* Dead:
A Psychic Medium Survives His Son's Suicide Through Spiritualism

Copyright © 2022 by Ron Pappalardo

ISBN: 978-1-7356932-9-3
ISBN: 1-7356932-9-4
Library of Congress Control Number: 2022901893

Cover Photo by Kozlak
Cover Design by Bill Van Nimwegen

Sacred Life Publishers™
SacredLife.com
Printed in the United States of America

To Connie,

my wife and best friend.

Contents

Introduction

In 2003, I lost my seventeen-year-old, first-born son, Joshua, to suicide. He had been suffering from clinical depression for years. Even though my wife Connie and I knew there was a possibility things might end this way, it was still no less of a shock when it actually happened. The traumatic experience turned my world upside down, and launched me onto an unusual years-long voyage. Part of the journey involved traveling to cities and countries I'd never been to before, but most of it was an internal one, a movement of the heart and spirit. It was initiated by my strong desire to find out if my son continued to exist in some kind of afterlife, and to know whether or not he was at peace and doing well.

As I watched my son lying in his hospital bed, slowly slipping away, my thoughts turned to questions of what would happen to him after his soul left his body. My Roman Catholic upbringing taught me that a suicide would be consigned to flames of eternal damnation. Joshua would receive unending torment for the *mortal sin* of taking his own life. My heart screamed that this could not be the case, that a loving God would not treat his children that way. Nevertheless, I was still full of anxiety. I suspected that even if there was no such thing as an eternal Hell, Josh might still be in some spiritual realm where he would be in distress and in need of assistance. If there was anything I could do from this side to help him, I just had to find a way to do so.

There was also the issue of my own need for help, something I was oblivious to at the time. The good news is that my focus on finding and helping my son caused me to embark upon a path that unintentionally led to my healing.

Some of the things I've learned along the way have challenged my beliefs to the core. What I discovered was of such a startling nature that I would often walk around the house in astonishment with my mouth agape. As a result, I had to completely revisit my entire belief system. I've had to discard many beliefs I held to be true and embrace new insights that I could have never imagined.

It was with some trepidation that I started this book, worried that my words might appear quite unbelievable or strange to the reader. Nevertheless, I feel compelled to reveal what I've learned. Let's face it. The belief systems that humanity has embraced for the past few thousand years have not been very effective in producing a world of peace or social harmony. Perhaps it might be a good time to explore some different and new ideas.

As a result of Josh's passing, I took a renewed interest in the subject of life after death. In particular, I wanted to know if it was possible to establish communication with him on the "other side." Within just a few weeks I discovered that not only was this possible, but I found several people who received messages from Josh and passed them along to me. The messages were *evidentiary*, which means they contained information in them proving that they were coming from Josh. They relayed facts and details which would have been impossible for anyone other than me to know about. Some of these messages will be revealed for the first time here in this book.

The communications were of such a powerful and compelling nature that I began to wonder if I could also cultivate the ability to communicate with my son and others in the world of spirit. This possibility led me to join a Spiritualist church, enroll in a Spiritualist seminary and embark upon a years-long course of mediumship development. To my great joy, I discovered that I could also communicate with the so-called "dead," and I have used my gifts to enable hundreds of people to make contact with deceased loved ones, providing comfort and peace to the grief-stricken.

In this book I aspire to describe the world of mediumship in such a way that people can easily understand. I hope to shed some light upon and dispel some of the misconceptions surrounding this little understood realm of human activity, a practice that has been with us since prehistoric times. I will also share some of the experiences I have had with Joshua since he "crossed over" to the other side.

This book expands upon the foundation of my first book, *Reconciled by the Light: The After-Death Letters from a Teen Suicide*. Since that book's publication in 2010, I have been exposed to a whole new world of learning and experiences.

1 - From Broken to Healed

When the police officer called me just after Josh's accident, which turned out to be not an accident at all, he wasn't that concerned. He told me he was pretty sure that my son would be able to recover from his injuries. After all, the ambulance had arrived within a few minutes, and the emergency medical technicians were already treating him before he even reached the hospital. Sadly, the policeman's hopes were unfounded.

A few hours later Connie and I found ourselves standing by his hospital bed looking at the screens on the monitors. We watched helplessly as his heart started beating slower, and slower, and slower, and finally stopped altogether.

Even the doctors were surprised that Joshua drifted away so quickly. Knowing him the way I did, I was not. Josh's clinical depression ran so deep that he had lost the will to live many months prior to his fatal decision. Psychotherapy and medications were powerless to stop his descent into hopelessness.

At one point, Josh shocked me by asking me if I would help him take his life. Of course, I refused, but imagine the feeling in the heart of a father whose son has just asked him to help him die. I felt like a complete and utter failure as a father and as a person. Helpless, bewildered, full of anxiety, desperate; I felt all of this and more.

If I hadn't been able to make contact with Josh through mediumship, I wouldn't be the person I am today. I would have remained broken in heart and in spirit. I am so grateful that I found this ancient practice. It led me out of my dark yesterdays and into many bright todays and tomorrows.

I cannot give a complete picture of Connie's path, but I can say that her healing process took longer and was more painful than mine. Nevertheless, she did not allow herself to falter in her duties as a wife and mother. She felt it was vital that she continue to fulfill her responsibilities to our surviving children, showing them an example of staying strong in the face of adversity. Connie is an artist and being able to throw herself into such a creative outlet was very therapeutic for her. Some of her paintings during this time were a reflection of what she was going through as a mother having lost her first-born child.

I can also say with confidence that her path paralleled mine in important ways. She accompanied me on many of my visits to spiritualist churches, mediums, speaking engagements, suicide prevention programs, and the many workshops and seminars I have taught. Her support for my work, which didn't take long to become *our* work—was immeasurable. Along the way she also developed her spiritual gifts, and on some occasions, we have both encountered the spirit of Josh at the same time. It is totally accurate to say that mediumship played a vital role in her healing process as well as mine.

2 - What About Evil Spirits?

People often ask me if I fear "evil spirits" when I practice mediumship. They are usually surprised to hear me say that it's not a major concern of mine. In my practice of mediumship, I have encountered spirits that I would describe as ignorant, regretful, and/or uncooperative, but I can't recall an encounter with a spirit I would describe as "evil." That's not to say that they don't exist, it's just that I have not encountered them.

I think the reason for this is fairly simple. My motivation and intention for practicing mediumship is helping people. A session with a medium is called a *reading*, and the person receiving the reading is called the *sitter*. I begin each session with a prayer in which I ask my "angels and spirit guides" to be present, and ask that everything that might transpire be for the *highest good* of those involved—the sitter and everyone they are connected to both here on earth and in the spirit world. I ask for the Holy Spirit to come and surround us with the bright white light of Divine love and wisdom. I think that having a good intention and starting with this type of prayer provides protection from negative energies.

What happens when I engage in mediumship is that I am raising my vibration higher while the good entities in the spirit world are lowering theirs. We are meeting somewhere in between. The higher vibration is not a comfortable space for potentially invasive lower entities.

It's like a story I heard about a group of troublemaking youths in a shopping mall who were bothering people and got chased out by the security guards. They came back through another entrance and started all over again until someone came up with the brilliant idea of playing classical music through the mall's music system, and then they quickly left for good.

Having said that, I caution people to not enter into mediumship without the proper intention and preparation. Without this, it is possible to come under the influence of spirits that will not have the highest motivation and integrity.

The closest thing to an evil spirit that I ever encountered was during a reading I was doing for a woman. The reading was going very well. I was able to make contact with two or three people that this sitter wanted to communicate with. Towards the end of the session, she asked me if I could find one more person. She seemed to be a little ambivalent about it, but I went ahead and honored her request. I didn't sense the presence of anyone, so I asked her for a name. She gave me the name of a man, and I repeated it three times in my mind to see if that would help my guides locate him in the spirit world.

There was no response at first, and then, way over in a corner far to the left of my psychic vision, a man slowly and gingerly appeared. I was surprised by his appearance. He looked like a homeless person. He reminded me of the picture of the man on the cover of Jethro Tull's *Aqualung* record album. His hair was long and unkempt, he wore a scraggly beard, and his clothes looked extremely worn and tattered. His countenance was sad. He didn't look comfortable at all. He made no attempt to move closer to me and when I tried to engage him, he was unresponsive. I got the sense that he was mistrustful and feared talking to me. It seemed like he would rather just run away and hide. I was not successful in establishing any communication with him, and this disappointed me. I felt that it would have been to his benefit if I had been able to talk to him. I said to the woman, "I'm sorry, but this person isn't willing to communicate with me. The only thing I can say to you is, he's not a 'happy camper.'"

To my disappointment, the woman expressed no sympathy for this person's predicament. With an indignant air she replied, "Well, that doesn't surprise me. He hurt a lot of people when he was on the earth."

When I told this story to a friend he astutely asked "Who is the supposedly evil spirit in this story? The man who is so sad and withdrawn, or the woman who is holding the grudge and not forgiving him."

I have encountered more evil intent in people living on the earth than I have from "evil spirits." Some have attempted to use those of us who have gifts of spirit communication for selfish or ignoble intentions. One of their victims was a man called *Honi the Circle Drawer*. He lost his life because of such people.

Honi was a Jewish *holy man* who ended a drought with his prayers. The story is recorded in the *Mishnah*, a collection of Jewish teachings:

> *Once they said to Honi the circle drawer, "Pray that rain may fall."*
>
> *He prayed, but the rain did not fall. What did he do? He drew a circle and stood within it and said before God, "Oh Lord of the world, your children have turned their faces to me, for I am like a son of the house before you. I swear by your great name that I will not stir from here until you have pity on your children."*

Rain began falling drop by drop. He said, "Not for such rain have I prayed, but for rain that will fill the cisterns, pits, and caverns."

It began to rain with violence. He said, "Not for such rain have I prayed, but for rain of goodwill, blessing, and graciousness."

Then it rained in moderation, until the Israelites had to go up from Jerusalem to the Temple Mount because of the rain. They went to him and said, "Just as you prayed for the rain to come, so pray that it may go away!" [1]

In a later incident, the Roman Jewish historian Josephus writes that Honi was killed for refusing to use his spiritual gifts to cause harm to others:

Now seeing that this civil war would last a great while, he [Honi] had hidden himself, but they took him to the Jewish camp and desired that just as by his prayers he had once put an end to the drought, so he might in like manner call curses down on Aristobulus and his supporters.

And when, having refused and made excuses, he was nonetheless compelled by the mob to supplicate, he said, "O God, king of the whole world! Since those that stand now with me are your people, and those that are besieged are also your priests, I beseech you, that you will neither hear the prayers of those others against these men, nor to bring about what is asked by these men against those others." Whereupon the wicked Jews that stood about him, as soon as he had made this prayer, stoned him to death. [2]

---

[1] *Mishnah* Taanit 3:8.
[2] Flavius Josephus, *The Antiquities of the Jews*, 14.2.1.

3 - Finding My Dead Son

After Josh took his life, I was very concerned about what would happen to him when he arrived in the spirit world. Even though I no longer embraced the ideas about suicide that I was taught during my religious upbringing, I was worried that he might wind up in a place more like what the Catholics call *purgatory*. According to the *Baltimore Catechism* that I studied as a boy in parochial school, purgatory is a place where people go who are not yet good enough to get into Heaven, but not bad enough to be sentenced to Hell. It is a place where they will be purged and purified from their sins, and then be admitted into Heaven. A soul might spend many years in purgatory before being allowed to move on to a higher place. Catholics also teach that it's possible to shorten a soul's sojourn in purgatory if those of us left behind on earth pray and/or perform other beneficial actions for them.

The spirit that reminded me of *Aqualung* might be in a kind of purgatory. That's why I was disappointed by the attitude the woman for whom I did the reading had towards him. If she had been willing to pray for him or—better yet—find a way to forgive him, I'm convinced it would have improved his situation in the spirit world.

Both Connie and I were certainly praying for Josh after he left us, but I wanted to do anything else I possibly could to help him. I was more familiar with the subject of life after death than the average person. Over the years, I had read books like *Life After Life* by Raymond Moody and *Thirty Years Among the Dead* by Carl Wickland. The afterlife was something I had already been very curious about, but my interest became more urgent now that Josh had gone there. I needed to know if he was okay.

When I tried to think of someone who might be able to help me find a way to make contact with Josh, the Rev. David Hose came to mind. David is a long-time friend of mine who lives in the Seattle area. He had recently published a book related to spirit communication and I knew that in the course of working on that book he had come into contact with people who had the gift of mediumship. So, I called him up, and he referred me to Barbara Ten Wolde.

Barbara is a spiritually-gifted woman who was also living in the Seattle area. Within just a few days of reaching out to her I received my first report about Josh's status in the spirit world. Barbara had a vision of Josh standing with his shirt off in a pool of some kind of liquid—like water, but not water. He was surrounded by spirit entities who were gently and lovingly reaching down into the pool and then pouring the soothing liquid all over his body. I asked if she was able to have any direct communication with Josh. She said "No," that it was too soon for that, and I intuitively knew that he needed more time before he would be in any kind of state to be able to communicate with me.

I struggle to describe how much this simple report affected me. It was a huge relief. As horrific as it is to contemplate, the truth is that Josh had taken his life through self-immolation. He had sustained burns over 98% of his skin surface. It made sense that these angelic beings were performing this heavenly healing procedure upon him.

Even more than that, I was relieved to discover that Joshua was not in hell, or even in a place reflecting the traditional concept of purgatory. He appeared to be in a place of convalescence, a place of healing, a place of deep compassion and love. As a parent, I can't think of anything more comforting than this, knowing that my child is safe and being lovingly cared for.

4 - The Day We Buried Josh

After this first glimpse of Josh, we held his memorial service the following Sunday. The Rev. David Hose graciously agreed to fly out from Seattle to my home in Cary, North Carolina, to lead the service and give the eulogy. Just before the service, we had an amazing encounter with the spirit of Josh:

Sunday came, and the house was a zoo. Friends, high school kids, and neighbors swarmed, it seemed, over every inch of the house . . . David Hose's plane had come in the night before, and he slept in the family room downstairs. The house was overflowing with food, flowers, and messages of condolence.

A few hours before the service was to start, David came to me with a nervous look on his face.

"Ron," he said, "The service is at three o'clock and I haven't finished composing my talk yet. Have you got a quiet room where I could go to collect my thoughts?"

I looked into the living room—it was packed with guests. I knew it would be the same story in the family room.

"What do I do now?" I thought. "I don't want to kick people out, but David needs some space." Then it occurred to me that there was one place in the house that was very quiet—Joshua's room—but I thought David might be a little hesitant to go in there.

"David, would you feel comfortable using Joshua's bedroom? Right now, that's the only quiet place in the house."

"Sure," David replied enthusiastically. "That'll do just fine."

"It's the door in the back up there." I said, pointing to the upper floor of our split-level house.

"Thanks, Ron." With that he bounded up the stairs with his pen and pad in hand.

A few minutes later, he stuck his head out the door and called to me. "Hey Ron, could you come up here?"

Puzzled, I climbed up the stairs to Josh's room. David had closed the door behind him after calling to me, so I slowly opened it and stepped in. I found David kneeling very quietly on the floor. It seemed that he might be crying. "Ron, Joshua is here in the room right now," he said.

I stopped breathing. Stunned, I couldn't find anything to say for a moment. David was just sitting there motionless, in deep concentration. I could see the tears now on his cheeks.

"David, are you able to communicate with him?" I asked anxiously.

"I don't know. Give me a minute."

The minute seemed like an hour. Finally, David broke the stillness.

"He's in a lot of emotional distress right now, but I think—if we give him time – I think he has something he wants to say."

After another long moment passed, David spoke again—but he wasn't talking to me.

"Josh," he said, "In a couple of hours we're holding a memorial service for you. Is there anything you want to say to your friends?"

Another quiet pause, and then, David's voice gently broke the silence.

"He spoke," David said, his voice almost a whisper. "Just four words . . . very slowly. 'Don't . . . ever . . . do . . . this!'"

I opened the door and called for Connie to come up. After she joined us, Josh began to speak through David a little more. He seemed hesitant at first, as if he wasn't sure if he was even welcome in our house anymore. He was feeling a tremendous amount of shame and guilt, worried that he had deeply disappointed us. After a while I grabbed a writing pad and began to take notes. Unfortunately, I didn't get everything down. A lot of what Josh said has been lost, but here are some of the things I wrote down. At first it seemed he was responding to David's question; if he had been given a chance to speak directly to his teenage friends, this is what he would have wanted to say. The time was 12:40 p.m., August 17, 2003:

"I'm not gone."

"Don't forget me. I'm still here."

"You should know there's something beyond this life. I'm not saying you should go back to church, but you should live your life with the understanding that there's more to it after you die."

This was typical Josh. He had really soured on institutional religion, after having had some disappointing experiences.

"Dad, you have to tell my friends this, 'your clothes, what you wear, or whether or not you're popular doesn't mean shit!'"

Anyone who knows David Hose knows that he is the last person in the world who would have expressed himself like this. When I heard the word "shit" I said to David, "Now that really sounds like Josh."

Immediately Josh replied, "You can quote me on that." I couldn't help myself, and I laughed. What a bizarre situation. My son has committed suicide, and here I was sitting on the floor of his bedroom talking to him through spirit communication, laughing because he said the word "shit." They never covered *this* in Parenting 101.

David said that Josh had a strong feeling of regret, a feeling of failure. We comforted him and told him we loved him and weren't angry at him.

By this point we had been joined by his brothers Gabriel and Ari. His sister, Nadia, still hadn't emerged from her bedroom.

Again, through David, Josh said, "Tell Nadia I love her."

The last thing I wrote down was a question from me to Josh.

"Could you hear us when we were talking to you in the hospital room?"

I couldn't hear your words at the hospital, but I could *feel* them. I could feel the love. Right now, I can hear you really well."

This session with Josh lasted about twenty minutes. At the end he mentioned some beings from the other side that were trying to communicate with him.

"There are some people who want me to go with them. They seem like they're good, but I don't know any of these people."

I encouraged Josh to go with these entities. I thought they would escort him into a good place in the spirit world. This appeared to be a classic example of a somewhat earthbound spirit. In many other instances, the deceased will recognize familiar faces on the other side, such as parents, grandparents, or friends who have gone on before them. I was surprised that Josh couldn't recognize any of the spirits who were beckoning him and didn't know what to make of it. I thought it might be because there weren't many people he knew who had gone to the spirit world before him. His grandparents had both crossed over when he was very young, and he didn't know them that well. They lived in Florida, and we only managed to make a handful of visits before they passed on.

It also seems that many spirits will not ascend until after their memorial service. The service seems to play an important role in their ascension process.

Josh eased my mind when he finally said, "I'll probably go with these guides eventually."

He concluded with a simple housekeeping comment, addressed primarily to his siblings.

"Don't fight over my stuff; whatever you want to do with it is okay." With that, the communication ended.[3]

Ironically, this day of Josh's memorial service—a day that traditionally represents saying "goodbye" to a loved one—was more like a "hello." I felt that I had been reunited with my son, and this reunion was a more substantial experience than when he was alive. People who are suffering from depression are often withdrawn and difficult to communicate with, so this twenty-minute conversation with Josh was the deepest interaction I had with him in many months.

After the service, David said he would attempt to spiritually contact Joshua again the following morning before he had to leave to catch his plane back to Seattle. His attempt was successful, and this time I was ready to write down the message that David channeled from Josh, word for word. Some of Josh's friends were present at this breakfast meeting, and most of his words here seem like they were addressed primarily to them:

Message from Joshua
Morning of August 18, 2003

I want to express my thanks for all the love I received yesterday. It's not so easy for me to come right now because I have to make some

---

[3] Ron Pappalardo. *Reconciled by the Light: The After-death Letters from a Teen Suicide.* 2010. pp. 39-42.

adjustment, but it seems that because of all the love that's around me, I'm given this opportunity to express the gratitude I feel with all the overflowing love I experienced from you yesterday.

It's clear that I was surrounded by your love and the love of God. I should have been more sensitive to the way you felt about me when I was with you.

I think I've already learned something because being here makes things very clear. Thank you for your great love.

I stand here to wish you the best as you go on your journey, as I go on mine.

Don't waste time listening to the buzzing in your head. Do you understand? You know, the waves of negative thoughts that go on inside your head? I've learned I must rise above that. I'm in no position to give advice, but I want to say something more deeply than just "Don't ever do this." Please don't give in to those negative emotions. You are too precious to give in to those things.

All the help you need for your life is right there with you, on earth. You just have to look around you so you can see it. Your friends, your family . . . they're all there to help you.

Again, thanks. You helped me powerfully yesterday. Sometime soon I can be freer maybe. I want to be in contact with you, because you are the best people I know.

The message was short, but it was clear and to the point. I received great comfort from this message. It seemed that Josh would have to go through a period of processing the many thoughts and emotions that filled his heart and soul after such a traumatic end to his life and entry into a whole new world. Nevertheless, I got the sense that he was in a safe place and that he had the humility to receive guidance from those who sought to help him in the spirit world.

5 - Josh Sends a Letter from Heaven

A few weeks later, Connie and I received another message from Josh. We had requested this message a couple of weeks earlier from a woman in Texas who had a special gift for spirit communication. In her case, she just sat quietly in front of her computer. Then she would focus her attention on the deceased person and make contact with him on the other side. Sensing his presence, and then his thoughts, she channeled Josh's words by typing them into her computer. She then mailed us a transcript of this "letter" from him.

When the letter arrived, I wouldn't read it initially. I was afraid of what it might reveal. My biggest concern was that Josh might be angry with me. I was worried that he might view me as a failed father. He might ask, "Why didn't you save me from killing myself?" I wasn't sure I could handle such an accusation.

In truth, I did hold myself responsible for his death. I was his father, after all. Why wasn't I able to protect him? Why wasn't I able to provide him the help he needed? Why had I failed to prevent his death? These questions tormented me, and I didn't know what to expect when I read his letter.

I was also worried that Josh's anger would place him in a spiritual prison and feared that he would be trapped by his resentment, in a hell of his own creation, unable to escape the darkness and ascend to a higher place.

These were the thoughts I wrestled with as I contemplated reading his letter. I tried to muster up the courage to face his words. I waited until an opportune moment presented itself. Connie and the kids had to leave the house for some reason, so I would have the privacy I needed. After they had departed, I locked the front door, disconnected the phone, and retired to the protection of my bedroom. I locked its door as well; some reflex action giving me a false sense that I was now somehow more protected.

Then I prayed. "Dear God," I said, "I don't think I can handle reading this letter by myself. I need you to be with me right now; let us read this letter together."

I remember the feel of the envelope in my hand, opening it, taking out the few pages inside, sensing the texture of the paper and unfolding the two creases in the white letter-sized sheets.

Then I began to intently read:

Reading with Josh Pappalardo
September 24, 2003

This is the Council of Light. We want to express to the parents of Josh that we are just beings of heart who wish to create a bridge that can allow loved ones to communicate freely and casually between these worlds, the physical and the spiritual. So, we are here at your calling on their behalf as they seek communication with Josh.

Josh is here and we are with him now. He is a bright young man, bright as his parents truly know him to be, but not as he appeared in recent times leading to his passing. For this he has much regret. Not only that he was in a slump (as he calls it) for so long, but that they cannot see how truly bright he is now. We will let him speak as he is very able to communicate, and he is anxious to express himself to his family.

Mom, Dad, this is Josh. I am speaking with my heart, and I am so relieved that you can receive my words as if I am speaking them directly to you. I feel so much love and light and energy coming from you, and this totally is changing me. Well, it is not changing me so much as it is freeing me to be myself.

I want to begin by saying how sorry I am for putting you through this horrible, senseless experience. For me, it was "another day in the messed-up life of Josh," but I know that for you it was a real shock, and I can see that it has caused you so much pain. This burdens me, and I sincerely apologize. Please forgive me, and please forgive yourselves also because you really are not at fault. I made choices that were bad choices. That is the amazing thing about growing up. We reach a point in our lives where we can make choices, and we sometimes just make stupid ones that lead into more stupid ones, and it's all a downward spiral. Of course, I didn't see this when I was on the earth. I was just caught up in the emotions and the energy of rebellion. It was an addiction to rebellion. It gave me a sense of control and escape at the same time. What I didn't realize is that it was propelling me into oblivion! And so, this is where it brought me.

I wish that I could say that everything is all right and I am happy, but you know that I am not. Just as you are suffering, I am too. I have to face what I have done, which is a big violation of the gift of life, and it is a slap in the face of those who created me. I was born of love—yours, God's, the whole universe's. And I snuffed out my life on earth in a moment of thoughtlessness. This is hard to reconcile, and it causes me great pain. I also disrupted the lives of my younger siblings in ways that are difficult for anyone to comprehend, and I regret this deeply. I ask also for their forgiveness. Please, please know that I love you deeply and I am crazy about you. You mean all the world to me, and I would never have imagined that I could hurt you so by doing this before your eyes. Please forgive me, and please choose a good experience we had together and record this as the memory you had of us together, not those last months and hours I had on the earth. This will free my heart and allow me to feel your mercy. I need that from you so much.

So, this is what weighs so heavily in my heart — the family and friends whom I hurt through my stupid choices, my attitude, and my passing. I took my life, and no one should feel so proud before God and their parents as to feel that they have the right to do this. Mom and Dad, please don't try to just skim over these words from my heart because they may bring you pain and regret. I need to express this from my heart because it is what I am working through at this time. It is a road I must travel in the process of healing. I want to walk it with you. Please, please hear me. I love you so much, and I need you to feel this love because I know that in the last years and months, I have not expressed it to you. In my rebellion I tried to hurt the world back, and it was you who I was hurting. It was you, and I am so shocked to see what I was doing to you. How could I have been so blind in my heart not to see this?

(He cries at this point and is silent)

Dad, I am so proud of you as my father. I am so proud to be your son.

(He cries again)

The dark energy that I created through rebellion and attitude became darker and more powerful than me, it engulfed me. My soul was lost in this dark cloud of energy. It was like a tornado. I could not think, feel, or move inside anymore. I just got swept up in the power, the roar and confusion of the twister — and I was gone. I also turned everyone else's lives upside down. You were left to pick up the pieces after the storm.

I was dead a long time before I took my life. I died inside. It was like an implosion. I have to say that by the time I took my life I had no feeling of myself left to get in touch with, much less those around me. This is why I could do such a terrible thing. I just didn't feel anymore. I didn't start out this way. Please understand this, because I am just slowly piecing this together. I just started out trying to express myself and to create my identity separate from what I thought was false and wrong (with religion, society, the established traditions). But in the process, I fueled my ideas *with other energies. I eventually could not separate myself from those energies, and I was changing so fast, even for myself.*

Dad, can you do this for me? Can you please share this with my friends? I am not the only one in this space. Some of my friends are also caught up in this energy. Don't label it as "evil sources" because it turns people off. Just say it in my words.

It is energy we generate with our thoughts, attitudes, the things we read, listen to, and see that reinforces our negative thinking. Tell them to step back and breathe, be quiet with themselves and listen to their hearts. Tell them to not lose touch with their souls, who they truly are within. I was so surprised Dad to find that my soul was so bright deep inside. I could not believe this was me. I scarcely had a feel for myself in the end, and when I could, I only saw darkness. But that wasn't me. And the world around me was not all that bad. It was ME who was seeing only the bad. We create the reality around us. Please just share this with my friends, even if just one or two want to hear me out, please let them know that this is what happened to me. It does not have to happen to them. Not that anyone will be so stupid as to take their life. I know this took a lot of courage for me—stupid courage, but they don't need to live in such darkness. It is not necessary. Dad, don't be concerned about whether they accept this or not, just share it with them and anyone who may be struggling in a similar situation as myself. It is the truth, and it will speak to them deeply in their hearts if they are ready to hear it. I am close to my friends, and will try to convey this to them in other ways as well. It's just that it's so amazing to me that I can express it in words through this communication.

Mom, I love you, and I will always remember your love and your words of comfort as you tried to understand me, to reach me. We are still in touch with each other. Know this, that I am more present in your lives now than I have been in several years even though I was on the earth then. And I can talk to you directly, even without Ms. G.

I am getting the support I need here to grow and to rise above the issues that I have carried with me. It's all love here, no judgment. I am surrounded by very loving beings who tend to my needs and encourage me to venture outside of my shell that I had created for myself.

I want to tell you that I have met a young man named Andrew Byrne. He is such a good person, and he approaches me as if we have known each other forever. He puts his arm around me, and he shows me that he cares. He is so bright, and he also told me about his life and some of his mistakes. He says that he also had issues when he passed. He didn't take his life like me. He was careless (that means wild) he says, and he found himself here in a flash. He has helped me through this period of regret. It is so hard to rise above regret. But he is here with me often, and I am so grateful to him. Others come who passed in the same manner as I — by taking their own lives. Everyone's story is different, yet so similar. And no one judges me. They just bring love and encouragement. So, you should know that who I'm hanging out with on this side you would very much approve of. (He laughs)

I leave you now. My love to everyone and especially to my siblings. I appreciate everyone's prayers and light and love. This all gets translated into wonderful support in the form of uplifting thoughts and feelings that last. This is what sustains me — your love.

I wave good-bye to you. I feel I never said good-bye. This talk has lifted a heavy burden from my heart. I know that I was emotional and maybe heavy at times, but know that this has been very good for me — to express what was deep in my heart freely to you, and to know that you receive it with love. I also felt restless because I naturally wanted to communicate this message to my friends. I know that you will help me do this Dad. You always respected me. I know that you think you were probably not caring enough. But you just were upset at that "monster" that had become me, and very rightfully so. You were upset at me for allowing myself to let this monster of energy consume me. I understand this now.

Bye. Love. Josh.

I was doing well in the beginning, drinking in every word and fascinated by the phenomenon itself of receiving a letter from a deceased person. The introduction from the spirits who called themselves the *Council of Light* reminded me of a similar group of benevolent spirits called the *Mercy Band* who worked with Dr. Carl Wickland in the 1920s.[4]

I was struck at how genuine the letter was. Joshua was pouring out his heart and soul with deep feeling and raw emotion. The painful honesty and sincerity were undeniable. He seemed to have a newfound sense of humility. I was ecstatic to find that he had arrived at a place where he was willing to listen to others and learn with an open heart.

I got to the place where he paused and began to cry. Then he said the words my soul had been aching to hear:

Dad, I am so proud of you as my father. I am so proud to be your son.

Without warning, my emotional dam burst wide open:

> I wailed loudly as the feelings poured out from deep within my soul. Tears rolled down my cheeks and my nose ran and ran. Saliva even oozed from my mouth. I became a soggy mass of wet. Meanwhile, my stomach churned inside my gut, the muscles becoming sore from the intense contractions. The noise of my wailing would probably have been disturbing to anyone who would have heard it. I grabbed a pillow and buried my face in it to mask the sound—my wailing was so loud I thought someone might call the police.

---

[4] Carl A. Wickland, M.D. *Thirty Years among the Dead.* Van Nuys, California: Newcastle Publishing Co., Inc. 1974. pp. 34-35.

The agony of the years of stress and anxiety over the struggle to save my boy gushed out like the water that flows from an open fire hydrant.

The spectacle of a grown man in the depths of grief is an awesome sight. I've seen pictures from Iraq of masculine, middle-aged men grieving over a dead son—eyes bloodshot, faces twisted in anguish, liquid oozing from every orifice. This is what I must have looked like. It had been over a month since Joshua had passed, yet I was only now allowing myself the opportunity of letting it all out, and even though it hurt, it hurt in a good way.

Within the cascade of jumbled emotions, two stood out above the rest. They emerged like two mighty stones protruding from the middle of a swirling whirlpool, offering me refuge from the flood—forgiveness and liberation.

I hadn't been able to escape the thought that maybe this had all been my fault, that if I had somehow done something different, Josh would still be with us. I thought Josh might be blaming me from the other side, caught up in a bitter anger at the father who failed him.

Furthermore, I was concerned that if he were harboring such resentment, it would be a shackle for him. Now I knew that he was not bound by such chains. He was free, and because he was free, I was also free. I felt the joy of liberation beginning to soothe my soul.

If he could say, "I'm proud to be your son" it meant that from the other side he now understood what I had gone through. He now knew the efforts and sacrifices that both Connie and I had made to try and help him. He saw the sleepless nights, the prayers, the frustration at not being able to reach him.

Along with liberation I felt forgiveness. I could start to forgive myself, and I knew that Joshua had forgiven me as well. In the days and weeks that followed, I would start to love myself again.

After several minutes, I slowly began to calm down. The reservoir of grief poured itself out and began to taper off, quietly ebbing away. In a few more minutes it was all over, and it felt as if I had arrived at the beginning point of my healing.[5]

Healing also came through a series of dreams I had during the first few weeks after Josh crossed over that shared a common theme of reconciliation in progressive stages. In the early dreams, he would just drift into the dining room of the house with the family gathered together like nothing had happened, but he wouldn't interact with anyone. Then the dreams would progress to ones in which we looked at each other but exchanged no words. In later dreams, words of greeting would be exchanged and might include a light touch or a hand on the shoulder. In the last dream in this series, Joshua came right up to me, hesitated a little, and then reached out his arms to me. We fell into a full embrace, and the effect this dream had on me is indescribable. After this healing embrace, the series of dreams ended.

---

[5] Ron Pappalardo. *Reconciled by the Light: The After-death Letters from a Teen Suicide.* 2010. pp. 79-80.

6 - Josh's Story

Josh was born in Washington, D.C. on April 12, 1986. To this day, whenever I see the dogwoods and azaleas in bloom, I think about the time I drove him and Connie home from the hospital to our house in Falls Church, Virginia. Our street was ablaze with springtime color. It seemed like the whole universe was heralding and celebrating the birth of our beautiful baby boy.

I named him Joshua in honor of my two favorite people—Jesus (Jesus is a variation of Joshua; the name means, God is salvation.) and Joshua, the Old Testament leader who led the Israelites out of the wilderness into the Promised Land. I hoped that my Josh would be a blessing to humanity like these men had been.

Josh's birthday was also a second birthday for me. Before he was born, I was just a young man. The day he was born I became something new. I became a father. When I first beheld him, my heart exploded, and a love I didn't know I possessed gushed forth for the first time. I don't know how to explain it, but other fathers may understand. He was so beautiful to me.

He was perfectly formed—his face, his body. He had exquisite hands with long slender fingers. I told Connie, "I think he will have musical ability; he could be a talented pianist."

He was the easiest baby to care for. He slept through the night from the beginning, and he seldom cried for longer than to tell us he was hungry or needed a new diaper. He was nothing more than a bundle of joy and happiness.

When he was three months old, we moved to North Carolina. Within a few years he was joined by three siblings, Gabriel, Ari, and Nadia.

Josh seemed like a typical youngster, although he showed a delicate, sensitive side. He was full of physical vitality, but I think his social and psychological development lagged a bit.

In retrospect, there were two things that come to mind that might have been warning signs about what was to come. First, although he got along well with his siblings, Josh sometimes complained about the fact that he had so many brothers and sisters. He could be quite selfish with toys and things. I remember there were a few occasions where he told me, "You and mom had too many kids." We weren't a wealthy family, and I think he figured he would have more of everything if he had been able to remain the center of attention.

Second, on a couple of occasions when he was maybe two or three-years-old, he tried to push my mother-in-law down the half flight of stairs in the entryway of our home. She had moved in with us. He told her she should go away. I think he found her presence in the house a threat to his being the central object of attention. I found his insensitivity disturbing, but chalked it up to his being not much older than a toddler.

Josh kept his feelings inside. It was hard for Connie and me to get really close to him. He wasn't one to easily share his deeper self. Nevertheless, I can't say that he was very much different than the average kid. He did well in elementary school. He was an exceptionally intelligent student, and he was artistically talented as well. The school was small enough that the teachers knew him, the principal knew him, and the environment was safe for his fragile psyche.

Middle school was a disaster.

From the more intimate environment of elementary school, he was thrown into the cauldron of middle school. Instead of having one main teacher, he had a different teacher for each class. There were over 1,000 students, so it was impossible for either the teachers or the administrators to get to know them all.

He was bullied and made fun of. The richer kids ridiculed his clothes. I remember he came home one day in tears and disturbingly said, "Those kids, I hate them! I want to kill them all." Josh did not possess what the psychologists called coping skills. When he had a problem, he would withdraw, hide from it, and become quietly angry and alienated.

My second son Gabriel was the total opposite. He told Connie and me one day that he had been ridiculed sometimes in middle school for his clothing. At first it bothered him, but then he developed a coping technique. He would look directly into the eyes of his tormenter and calmly and confidently say, "Look at this face. Does it look like it cares?" He'd walk away, and the bullying soon stopped.

In time, Gabriel went on the offensive. An encounter went something like this:

"So, you don't like my shirt? I see you're working for Abercrombie and Fitch," he'd say.

"What do you mean?" the bully responded.

"Well, you spent twice as much as I paid for my shirt at Walmart, and now you're walking around advertising for Abercrombie and Fitch. They should be paying you, but you're paying them to give them free advertising."

The contrast between Joshua and Gabriel couldn't have been greater. I used to say to Connie that the assembly line that created the boys got stuck when Josh went through to get his dose of maturity. It skipped over Josh, and then gave Gabriel a double dose.

Even as he struggled, Josh displayed a hilarious sense of humor. He was often side-splittingly funny. He used to do voice impersonations. One of his best was his impression of a guy like Apu, the Kwik-E-Mart clerk in the Simpsons. Once he got that accent going, you would swear the kid had grown up in India. Then there was the time I took him to do a service project in Honduras when he was fifteen. Each group had to do a skit, and he played George W. Bush. His Texas accent and use of the term "Strategery" had me in stitches.

We had gone to Honduras as part of a project of the Religious Youth Service, one of my favorite charities. Teenagers from all over the world and local Hondurans worked with pickaxes breaking the stony ground to lay a foundation for a cultural center in a small town in the hills outside of Tegucigalpa. It was backbreaking work in the hot tropical sun. I noticed one day that Josh kept working while the other American and European kids had taken a break. Later in the day, I asked him about that.

"Dad," he said with genuine sincerity, "these little Honduran teenagers didn't take a break either. They live off of rice and beans. How could I, a big, strong, well-fed American, take a break? It just didn't seem right." To experience the heart that he had for those less fortunate than he was one of the proudest moments of my life.

After we found out about the bullying, we decided to get Josh out of the public school "student warehouse" and into a private Christian school. Connie got a job as a teacher's assistant there to help pay the tuition. We would pay for one child, and the other would be free. So, Gabe got to go as well.

The school used the Paideia system of education, which encourages a great deal of interaction between the teacher and the students in the classroom. Teaching is more individualized; the teacher does a lot of coaching and is open to assigning tasks to students based upon their own interests and input. Students are assessed as individuals and not in comparison to the group. Classes are sometimes little seminars, with the students included in group discussion. The boys thrived. They wore uniforms to school, so there were no clothing disputes. They enjoyed studying Latin, sang hymns, and got exposed to a God-centered culture, including prayers.

The boys told me they learned more in that one year than they had in all their public school years combined. Then the Paideia school fell apart. The founding couple divorced; after the school year ended, every teacher quit except one.

I looked into the possibility of a Catholic School, but the cost was beyond our budget. I struggled with the idea of putting Josh back in a public middle school.

Then his Latin teacher, who was also the principal at the Christian school, told me that Josh was probably intelligent enough to skip the eighth grade and go straight into high school. She was planning to leave the Paideia school to teach Latin at a new charter high school in Raleigh. He might follow her there with several of the other students. She suggested he take the SAT and see if he could score at least 1000, which was a pretty decent score even for a high school kid based on the scoring system that was in place at that time. He surpassed it, even though he was only in the seventh grade.

He started high school the next fall, but he didn't last. As the Latin teacher put it, he had the intelligence, but lacked the emotional maturity.

The only option left was to put him back in a public middle school. We did, but this time it was much closer to home, about a mile from our house. We had heard it was a good school. His life went slowly downhill from there. Josh became more and more distant, secretive, and rebellious. We're pretty sure it was around this time that he began smoking marijuana, although we have no proof.

When he got to high school, he took a strong interest in psychology. From his studies, he was convinced that he had a chemical imbalance in his brain. He diagnosed himself as clinically depressed. He asked if he could see a psychologist in hopes of getting some medication. I remember that the psychologist was skeptical.

"Our son believes he is suffering from depression," Connie had told him while calling to set the appointment.

"Well," he replied. "It will probably take several sessions before I am able to make that assessment one way or the other."

After only one visit, the psychologist concluded Josh was indeed clinically depressed and immediately set up an appointment for Josh to see a psychiatrist. The psychiatrist prescribed an antidepressant, Effexor, which seemed to help—at first. We didn't know at the time that Effexor increased the possibility of suicide. Not long after Joshua took his life, Effexor was no longer prescribed for young people his age.

After a few weeks, he stopped taking it. He said his friends told him he "wasn't himself" anymore. He didn't like the way it made him feel, like a zombie, with no feeling inside. We were never able to get him to take it, or any other medication, again.

Josh would sometimes shock us with the things he would say. "I'm not going to live to be thirty," he said a couple times. The most disturbing comment was, "I'll probably go out in a blaze of glory."

There was one very bright spot in his last couple of years of life. He met a wonderful girl his sophomore year and fell head-over-heels in love with her. The feeling was mutual. I never saw him as happy as when he was with her. He made a valiant effort to tame his demons and do well in school as well as work part-time after school, largely due to the fact that he wanted to be successful in her eyes. The relationship lasted exactly a year.

After they broke up, Joshua's depression roared back with a vengeance, which is often the case for young men with aching hearts.

One morning around 5 am, Connie was awakened by a cry of distress coming from Josh's bedroom. "Mom . . . mom . . . mom" came the troubled plea for help. Opening his door, Connie found him sitting up in bed, his back and head leaning against the wall.

"What's the matter, Joshie?" she asked.

"Mom. I had a bad nightmare." He was breathing heavily and looked terrified.

"There was this searchlight in the sky, moving all around, looking for me. I was trying to escape it, but eventually it found me. When the light hit me, I couldn't move, or talk, or even breathe. It was so scary. Then I woke up."

"Why don't you lay down and I'll rub your back." This was something Connie and I had done for Josh innumerable times before. Often the only way to calm him down and get him to sleep was to rub his back, sometimes for a half an hour or more.

Afterwards, Connie went back to sleep and had a dream with Josh in it. The terrified Josh had transformed into one that was happy and excited. He was giving Connie a tour of his new life.

"Look at my new house," he said, smiling.

He was dressed in his usual black hoodie and pants, but his demeanor was different. He was jovial, kidding around and expressing sincere affection for his mother, which was a rare experience for Connie in those days. He showed her around a house not much different from our own. He seemed proud of his new dwelling, and enjoyed sharing it with his mom.

The scene changed suddenly, and they found themselves inside an ice skating rink. Connie was leaning over the railing watching while Josh glided over the ice with glee. He was dancing—almost flying—along the ice, smiling broadly in total freedom.

A week later, he was dead.[6]

---

[6] Ron Pappalardo. *Reconciled by the Light: The After-death Letters from a Teen Suicide.* 2010. pp. 50-55.

Joshua's second birthday—
I thought he must be the happiest child in the world.

Joshua fell asleep while drawing, crayon still clutched in his
hand. I carried this picture with me for years, calling it
"Artist at Work."

Happy days! I'm holding my third son, Ari. Gabriel is on the left, Josh is in the middle, and my wife, Connie, is holding baby Nadia.

Joshua's Middle School Picture

*Joshua at fifteen – in Honduras for a Religious Youth Service
Project. Typically, he did something out of the
ordinary to his hair.*

*In hindsight, some pictures strike me as revealing a psyche
that wasn't quite right. Compare this picture of Josh with
the Honduras one, and the next one,
and note especially the eyes.*

Joshua having a great day at the beach,
just a few months before he died.

7 - Mediumship: The Oldest Spiritual Path

Twenty-first century America contains a wide variety of religions reflecting the diversity of the people who now live here. Within a few miles of my home in Cary, North Carolina, stand houses of worship from the traditional Christian denominations such as Baptist, Methodist, and Roman Catholic, but more recent additions to my community reveal the presence of immigrants who have arrived here in just the last few years. Chatham Street now boasts a huge mosque constructed to serve the Muslim community, some of whom are refugees from the recent wars in Syria, Iraq and Afghanistan. On Chapel Hill Road some local Indians are adding a tower to their Hindu temple that is more than five stories tall. In this growing city of over 170,000, I have met people from every faith tradition imaginable, from Buddhists and Jews to Taoists and Zoroastrians. Even though the buildings, rituals, and belief systems might be different, these religions can all trace their origins back to the same phenomenon—mediumship.

Simply put, mediumship is the practice of establishing communication between people living on the earth and entities who dwell in a place variously referred to as Heaven, the spirit world, or the afterlife. Most religious movements began when someone living on the earth had an encounter with some intelligence living in the spirit world. For example, Judaism began when a man named Abram heard a voice that told him to move his family more than four hundred miles south to a land where "all peoples on earth will be blessed through you."[7] Christianity began when a man named Jesus heard a voice tell him "You are my Son, whom I love; with you I am well pleased."[8] Islam began when a man named Muhammad heard a voice telling him to "Read.[9]"

In all of these cases, humans experienced what mediumship calls *clairaudience*. The word is French in origin, and simply means "to hear clearly."

Prehistoric forms of mediumship go by a different name – *shamanism*. Even before the invention of writing, humans all over the world were burying their dead and appealing to those who dwell in the spirit world to receive their deceased loved ones with benevolence. In every tribe in every corner of the world there were those who had the gift of being able to communicate between the worlds of the living and the dead. Their names were different, but their practices shared many similarities. In ancient Greece one would consult the *Oracle of Delphi* for spiritual guidance. In the land of ancient Israel, they were called *prophets*. If Native Americans had problems that concerned the spirit world, they went to the *medicine man*, while in sub-Saharan Africa natives would consult the *witch doctor*.

All of these spiritually gifted individuals were practicing various forms of shamanism. Even though we can trace it back to prehistoric times, shamanism is still practiced today in places as far flung as Siberia, Korea, Africa, and in places where Native

---

[7] Genesis 12:3 *The Holy Bible. New Revised Standard Version* (NRSV). Peabody, Massachusetts: Hendrickson. 2004.
[8] Mark 1:11 (NIV)
[9] Quran 96:1

Americans still gather to participate in rituals such as the *sweat lodge* or the *vision quest*. Yet there are certain features that are common to all shamanistic traditions.

First, as in the case of the prophetess who enabled King Saul to communicate with the spirit of the prophet Samuel in ancient Israel,[10] the shaman serves as a channel to establish communication between the physical world and the spiritual world. Sometimes this communication changes the course of history, as when Joan of Arc's voices convinced the dauphin of France to allow her to lead his army in battle to defeat the English, or when Nettie Colburn's spirit guide convinced Abraham Lincoln to enforce the *Emancipation Proclamation*.[11] More often the shaman, medium, or prophet simply provides comfort to a grieving parent, as happened when I was given messages from Josh shortly after his passing.

The second reason people might consult a shaman is for healing, be it spiritual or physical. Notice that the Native American term for a shaman is medicine man, while the African term is witch doctor; *medicine* and *doctor* are, after all, terms associated with healing. In ancient times it was accepted that many physical ailments had an unseen or spiritual factor needing to be addressed. For example, when a child became sick in pre-Western Hawaii, the shaman, called a *kahuna*, would often check to see if there was some conflict in the family by talking to the various members. If she discovered that someone had hurt the heart and feelings of another, she would ask that person to reconsider and apologize for the offense. Then she would ask all the other members of the family to forgive the offender, which would consequently facilitate the recovery of the afflicted child. In other cases, the shaman might receive an intuitive direction that a specific food or herb might facilitate healing from a particular illness. Shennong, the father of

---

[10] 1 Samuel 28: 3-25 (NRSV)

[11] Nettie Colburn, *Was Abraham Lincoln a Spiritualist?* Philadelphia. Rufus C. Hartranft, publisher. 1891. p. 72.

Chinese herbal medicine who lived in prehistoric times, is called the *Divine Farmer*, suggesting that some of the knowledge he gained about medicinal herbs was inspired by Heaven.

A third reason people might consult a shaman is for help controlling the weather, like the Israelites did when they appealed to Honi the Circle Drawer to bring rain. In Native American tradition, tribesmen perform a shamanistic ritual called the *rain dance* during times of drought. Rain dancers are not limited to North America; farmers still employ them to produce rain in various parts of the world. Perhaps the most well-known story of a human controlling the weather is when Jesus commanded a storm on the Sea of Galilee:

> *A furious squall came up, and the waves broke over the boat, so that it was nearly swamped. Jesus was in the stern, sleeping on a cushion. The disciples woke him and said to him, "Teacher, don't you care if we drown?" He got up, rebuked the wind and said to the waves, "Quiet! Be still!" Then the wind died down and it was completely calm. He said to his disciples, "Why are you so afraid? Do you still have no faith?" They were terrified and asked each other, "Who is this? Even the wind and the waves obey him!"* - Mark 4:37-41 (NIV)

Another example of an ancient shamanistic practice of controlling nature that is still widely used today is called *dowsing*. It is used to find hidden underground reservoirs of water or other substances. The *dowser* is a person who is sensitive to the energy given off when he stands above such a reservoir. He uses a forked stick called a *divining rod*. The dowser walks back and forth across an open field, pointing the tip of his divining rod towards the ground, and when he passes over a place where there is underground water, his divining rod begins to vibrate and shake. Then a well is dug, revealing the water underneath.

Communicating with spirits, healing, and help with the weather or other natural forces are the three main reasons people would consult a shaman. Today, people most often consult a medium in order to communicate with someone in the spirit world.

8 - Josh Writes Again

The letter I received from Josh in September of 2003 was the main catalyst for my healing. It wasn't the only letter Connie and I received. A couple of months later we received another through the medium in Texas. We had been missing Josh terribly, and the woman, whom we will refer to as Ms. G. in order to protect her privacy, agreed to try and contact him again for us:

Reading with Josh Pappalardo
December 6, 2003

Hi, this is Josh. Thanks for seeking me out today, Ms. G. And thanks also for taking the time to open this communication for the sake of my parents. I have been waiting at your door for some time, and I hope you are not mad at me, but I knew you would try to reach me, and I wanted to be ready. I know how busy you are, so I appreciate this.

Hi Mom and Dad. Hi to everyone! I know you think that I am somewhere far away, but you would be so amazed to discover that I am right here with you. There is not like distance between us in space, but distance in consciousness. In other words, the distance is really in our minds. *Isn't it that way with so many things—just distortions of the mind! So much has happened since I last sent my communication to you. For me here, every day is a day of new discoveries. I am willing to change, so just to have that willingness affords me many opportunities for growth and new experiences. Not that it is easy. I am challenged in so many ways. If I have a gripe toward my parents for how you raised me as your son, it is that you made life too easy for me. This may be a shock to my younger brothers and sister, but it is the truth. I realize that I was very sheltered in my life and I knew nothing of what it was to do without and to suffer and to give. Here, we grow only by giving of ourselves, by putting ourselves out there for others. It is the same on the earth, but we just don't understand it as this. We think on the earth that intellect and money and position in society are what give us value. But that is not true. It just is the furthest thing from the truth. I am not saying that everyone thinks this way, or that this is how you taught me. All I am saying is that is what I thought and believed. And this is how most people I encountered lived.*

Here, we are stripped down to our soul, and nothing outside of this has much bearing on who we are or what we do. And so, I discovered that I am just a child. Mom and Dad, I was just a child. I thought I was all grown up, but I was just a little boy, acting out in the body of a young adult. Coming to this awareness was very sobering to me. If you need me to translate this into earth years so you have an idea how young I was emotionally and spiritually, I would say I was about six or eight years. Now, I can see my dad nodding and going "No wonder!" (He chuckles here).

So, this is how I started my life on this side, so young. You will be very happy to know that I am growing fast here. I have no idea how old I would now be in earth years, but I am no longer hanging out with the "kiddies" around here. That should give you some hope. (He chuckles again). We don't go by calendars and clocks around here and we don't have physical form that shows age. We just are.

In talking with my friends here who came to this side in the same manner as myself, we all agree that were we mature to the level where we are now in our age, we would never have made this decision to take our lives as we did. And so, our conclusion is that we are just not educated properly on the earth about what really matters in life, which is our emotional and spiritual development. If half the energy were devoted to this that is now devoted to the concerns of where we stand in society and who we are and what people think of us, we would soon outgrow all these stupid concerns because we would just "grow up!" I know I was a kid when I passed to this side, but at least I was still just a young person. Many people come here as full-grown adults, and they are just kids as well. Imagine their shock.

These are just my observations. You know me, always thinking these things through and trying to make sense of everything. I just can't let go of something until I figure it out and it seems right and just. These were sources of great frustration for me on the earth. I just could not understand so many things. I couldn't put two and two together, and I became disillusioned with life and with people, even with my parents, whom I looked up to and loved deeply. Now you can understand that I was just a little boy trying to understand this stuff. I was trying to put a puzzle together, but I did not have all the pieces of the puzzle, nor did I have a clear image of the puzzle itself. I often felt that somehow things that seemed to be so important to me didn't seem so relevant to others around me. This frustrated me deeply, and it made me irritated and angry. I am saying this in the first tense now, but it seems as if I am talking about another person. I have changed so much.

Ms. G is eating popcorn as she takes this dictation, and this amuses me. It's okay with me. I think it helps her keep going, but what she doesn't realize is that I was having a desire for popcorn, and she just walked over and she just got into it! (Note from Ms. G: He chuckles, and I realize that I never eat when I take dictation, but I did this so naturally, and then have consumed a whole bowl of it in a flash!)

And so, my life on this side is all right. I am at peace. I am not so anxious and hyper as when I last spoke to you. I actually feel more settled, and I am gaining a better sense of myself and my surroundings. I also have freedom to move out of this area where I live. Many who pass to this side turn right around and start helping others. I am not there yet. I am still being cared for and taught, because you know, I was just a boy. Andrew visits me often and I have made many new friends here.

And talking about friends, Dad, thanks for sharing my words with my friends. I am taking care of them. In a way, I also feel responsible because I had very weird ideas, and I think that I may have poisoned the minds of some of my friends by sharing my stupid thoughts. So, I was so glad when you could share "my reflections from the other side" (he chuckles) with them. I also feel responsible for some of the issues of my younger siblings because I think that I may have contributed to their problems. Dad and Mom, please know that I am taking care of my younger brothers and sister. I am being a good older brother to them, and you will see that it makes a difference in their lives in the long run. Don't make their lives difficult just because I said you were too easy on me. That was just me. You would really ruin my relationship with them. (And he chuckles again)

Mom, I know that with time you will become so aware of how close I am with you that you will not miss me anymore. This is a good way to grow and develop the gift of moving in and out of the two worlds—the physical and spiritual, because I am on this side and we can communicate. I am doing very well. Maybe it helps you to pretend that I am away at school (which is sort of true), and we will see each other again soon (which is true). The heart is very amazing. You can play tricks on it like this and it works. Try it.

I give my love to everyone, and now that Christmas is coming, I want to tell you that I will visit you and share this season with you as a shining bright star. You will know it is me when I visit you in this time. Let's have a happy Christmas. Please don't be sad. I feel so responsible for making your lives so difficult in the last few months since I made the decision to take my life. We all (who have done this) search in vain for ways to heal the wounds we cause to our families when we take our own lives in this way.

I love you all very much.
Josh

Note from Ms. G: Josh was very candid and light-hearted. He seems so much in control of his life and he appears to be very self-satisfied. A lot of it may come from his coming to finally understand issues that he couldn't figure out on earth (as he expresses). It was a real joy to do this reading with him, so different from the last time, which was all tears.

You can imagine how happy Connie and I were to read this beautiful letter. Aside from the fascinating content describing Josh's life and progress made in the spirit world, there is an amusing element to this message.

When Joshua was on earth, he loved microwave popcorn. He ate so much of it that we dedicated an entire drawer in the kitchen to nothing but packets of microwave popcorn. It wasn't unusual for fifteen bags at a time to be in there. He went through this stuff like locusts through a wheat field.

On another occasion, he identified himself through a medium by alluding to his "addiction" to microwave popcorn. I even referred to him as "the popcorn boy." So, Connie and I were startled when we read about popcorn in this message. It made the message sound even more genuine by adding this little evidentiary piece of information.

A second point is it appears that spirits can get vicarious satisfaction out of things we do on the earth plane. I know it sounds a little creepy, and I don't know the mechanics of how it happens, but it is true that alcoholic spirits will influence people on earth to drink, and the spirits of people who were addicted to drugs can influence people on earth to take drugs as well. So, I'm sure Josh influenced Ms. G to make some popcorn right in the middle of the reading with her! I imagine he really enjoyed "sharing" some popcorn with Ms. G, because I don't know if he can have the same microwave popcorn experience in the spirit world.

9 - Comfort for the Bereaved

When I was studying mediumship through the Morris Pratt Institute, a Spiritualist seminary in Milwaukee, Wisconsin, we were asked to consider just exactly what is the purpose and value of mediumship. Many people are attracted to mediumship simply because they are curious to investigate what they see as a strange— if not somewhat macabre—practice of communicating with the so-called dead. Others are fascinated by the myriad phenomena that can occur during what some refer to as *seances* and others call *spirit circles*. From hearing the voice of a medium change while channeling a particular spirit, to viewing small sparkling lights shimmering in the air in a darkened seance room, or experiencing physical phenomena like rapping on the wall or the clearly heard sound of disembodied footsteps walking by them, it is understandable that many people are drawn to experience the wide variety of manifestations of spiritual phenomena that can and do take place during spirit communication.

However, mediumship is much more than parlor entertainment or a demonstration of unusual happenings for curiosity's sake. At Morris Pratt I learned that more than anything else, there is a very profound and sacred purpose for mediumship. It is to bring solace to the hearts of people who have had their hearts broken from the pain of the separation that is felt through the passing of a loved one. Unless one has experienced it, it is simply not possible to understand the agonizing grief felt by, for example, a bride whose husband was accidentally killed just days after their beautiful wedding day, or the mother whose teenaged daughter wasted away from cancer before her very eyes, or the father whose son was killed on a battlefield in a faraway war.

I can never forget about the mother who almost went insane after losing most of her children in less than a week to a flu epidemic in the days just before Christmas. She had baked cookies for the upcoming holiday celebration. When her children asked if they could have one, she told them they would have to wait until Christmas Day itself. Tragically, they had passed away by then. She had a hard time forgiving herself for denying them the joy of eating one of her freshly-baked Christmas cookies before they died.

I think about the daughter who suddenly lost both parents in a fatal car accident, and a grieving son who was wracked with guilt because he wasn't able to make it home in time to be at his mother's bedside when her life drifted away.

In these and many other cases, mediumship can be the life preserver that provides the difference between anxiety and peace, insanity and wholeness, suffering and healing. I know that such was the case for me, and for countless others that I have worked with.

In my case, the grief I experienced stemmed from a feeling of separation. My son was suddenly gone. His room was empty, and he would never return. His high school bookbag lay on the floor, never to be picked up again. I would never again recognize the distinct footsteps he made as he entered the house when he came home from school and climbed up the stairs to his bedroom. I would never again know that secret feeling of relief a parent cherishes when they know their child has returned and is safely home once again.

One of the most terrifying thoughts I can think of is the idea, "My loved one is dead, and I will never see them again." For me, mediumship demonstrates that not only is my loved one still alive in the world of spirit, but I will definitely see him when my time comes to cross over into the next life.

There are other reasons why mediumship is of inestimable value to the human experience. One is eliminating the fear of death, and another is providing clear evidence of survivability—the idea that human consciousness survives and continues after the demise of the physical body.

I used to be afraid of death, but no longer. The more I experience evidence of the afterlife, the more the fear of death fades.

Recently, I've been moved and inspired by studies of Hospice patients that have given rise to a new and largely unfamiliar terminology; *end-of-life visions* or *end-of-life experiences*. It is becoming more and more evident that people who are getting close to the end of their physical lives are often visited by residents of the spirit world. Many Hospice patients speak of experiencing spiritual entities.[12] They describe some as Angels, and others see and hear deceased loved ones—most often their mothers. Sometimes the spirits visit them directly in their rooms, while at other times they appear to them in dreams and visions. In the majority of cases, these experiences have a soothing and therapeutic effect on those who receive them. They assuage the anxiety some people experience as they approach the end of their physical life. Here is the testimony of a woman who wrote to my wife and me after having lost her mother during the COVID-19 pandemic:

---

[12] Christopher Kerr. *Death Is But a Dream: Finding Hope and Meaning at Life's End.* New York: Avery. 2020.

After mom was in isolation for four months, seemingly happy, then out of nowhere she's fighting for her life with the Coronavirus. Last Thursday, May 28th, (2020) she told the nurse "I don't want to suffer anymore or be on a ventilator; I'm going to heaven tonight and want to see my kids one last time." The attending nurse allowed four of her six kids in to see her (wearing PPE) and her virtual goodbye party began. My mom said goodbye to thirty-nine family members through FaceTime and Zoom. She was So Happy! She kept saying, "I'm going to heaven tonight; they don't want me here anymore, because I have the coronavirus and pneumonia." They were the Angels in the room talking to my mom. We are believers, and mom knew exactly where she was going, and she was so excited.

10 - Not Evil, Just Stupid

End of life experiences are not the only encounters people have with spirits. I don't mean to cause alarm, but we all have spirit guides, angels, and other spirit entities around us influencing our thoughts on a regular basis. Whether we like it or not, spirits influence us. The good news is that most of the time they mean well, but sometimes their influence leads to negative consequences that were unintended. I am a living example of this.

I was born and raised in the Los Angeles area. People who know me well know that I was influenced by the laid back, "go with the flow" culture of Southern California. I've been described as a pretty open-minded guy, and I don't usually lose my temper or yell at people. My kids will tell you that I wasn't a very strict disciplinarian, and I didn't mind them climbing all over me or playing a game we called "the Flying Bambino Brothers." That was a game where I would lay on my back and hold onto their hands while lifting them high in the air with my feet. They loved it!

So, I was very surprised when they reached that age where they would talk back to me when I asked them to do something. I wasn't surprised that they did it; I was surprised at my reaction. On one occasion, I erupted in anger and started yelling at one of my boys for talking back to me. I was surprised because it was so out of character. A couple of weeks later, it happened again. I was shocked at the strong feeling of anger that welled up in me, and I talked to Connie about it. I told her I didn't feel like myself when this happened, so we began to suspect the influence of a spirit.

We have a friend named Christina Graham who has a gift for spiritual healing. She once told me that while she was performing her healing technique, she sometimes found spirits who were "attached" to her clients. She also told me that she found that she had the ability to detach these spirits and send them "to the Light." I called her up on the telephone.

"Christina, do you still do spiritual healings?" I asked. "I'd like you to come over and perform your healing service on me. I don't have a particular physical problem, but I would like you to be on the lookout for any spirits that are attached to me and see if you can remove them."

A few days later, Christina arrived and brought a massage table with her, just like the ones Reiki practitioners use. Then she had me lay down on it and made movements over me with her hands to facilitate healing. After the session was over, I asked her if she had found any spirits?

"Oh, yeah. There was one." she said. "I sent him to the Light. He didn't resist at all."

Then the "miracle" happened. The feeling of anger went away, and I never exploded on the kids again. It was stunning how complete the change was, but I was left wondering who the spirit was that had been causing the problem.

Later, the spirit's identity was revealed to me through spirit communication. His name was Mario Pappalardo. He was born in a small town in Sicily in the late 1800s, and he was my paternal grandfather. He had been with me for most of my life because he loved me and wanted to protect me. Even though I had never met him, I had made a close connection to his spirit when I was a young boy by making a special weeks-long prayer offering for his soul in front of a copy of the famous "Pieta" statue that was in my local Catholic Church.

When my grandfather saw my boys talking back to me, he became angry, because he loved me and was upset at how disrespectful the boys were being to their father. That would never be tolerated in Sicily. It was outrageous! That's the reason why I didn't feel like myself when these episodes happened. It wasn't my anger; it was his anger. American parenting in the twenty-first century is not like Sicily in the nineteenth century. When my grandfather was made aware that his good intentions were not welcome, he backed off, and never "jumped in" again. I'm sure my grandfather still has my best interests at heart and does anything he can from the spirit world to help me, but he's not invasive anymore.

The point of this story is that sometimes spirits have the best intentions but wind up causing problems. It reminds me of something one of my favorite spiritual mentors said, a Catholic nun named Sister Wendy Beckett. You may have seen her on PBS. She was a gifted art historian and analyst who had a hugely popular show produced by the BBC. More than anything else, Sister Wendy loved the contemplative life of her spiritual community, but on one occasion she agreed to be interviewed by Bill Moyers. He asked her if she was troubled by the fact that a lot of great art was sponsored by patrons who were, in his opinion, debauched sinful people. Sister Wendy replied, "They weren't sinful, just stupid, unin-structed." She said she had a great deal of compassion for them.

When people go to the spirit world, they carry their distinct personalities and beliefs with them, including their philosophies on parenting. My grandfather might have been judged by some as a wicked or evil spirit fuming with anger, when in reality he was a loving grandfather concerned for my well-being as his grandson.

11 - Unburdened

A reading I've never forgotten about was one I gave over the phone while sitting in my car in a church parking lot. Connie and I were traveling to some event far from home, and I hadn't covered enough miles to make it possible to do the reading in a more comfortable setting. However, that's not the reason I remember this reading. I remember it vividly because the content was so profound and illuminating to me.

The sitter was a woman living in Texas working in some sort of law enforcement job. She had a close relationship with a man employed by the oil industry who had been murdered. Because she was in law enforcement, she felt a special responsibility to do everything she could to bring his killer to justice. She was hoping that if I could contact him in the spirit world, he would be able to tell her who the murderer was.

I was able to find her friend in the spirit world, but what he had to say deeply surprised the both of us. He said that he wasn't at all interested in settling scores. He couldn't care less whether or not his killer was ever found out or arrested. He said that his life in the spirit world was so wonderful, and that his surroundings were so beautiful, that this was the last thing on his mind.

He advised his woman friend to just let the whole thing go. He said that he felt bad that she felt burdened by her sense of duty. He wanted to release her from this burden.

In its entirety, it was one of the most moving readings I've ever given. I've had similar sentiments expressed by many of the spirits I've been able to communicate with on the other side. They have emphasized how beautiful the spirit world is, how much peace and tranquility they have found there, and how little they are concerned with "getting even" with those who may have hurt them in the past. They are far more interested in exercising forgiveness and reconciliation, and it seems even more important to them that they receive forgiveness from anyone they may have hurt during their earthly lives.

12 - Can Spirits See You When You're Naked?

Now that I practice mediumship myself, I have discovered that doing so can lead me into some uniquely awkward situations difficult to explain later. For example, I was taking a shower one morning when I heard Connie's voice calling to me through the bathroom door.

"Ron," she said. "Mike is on the phone from Florida and wants to talk to you urgently. It sounds pretty important. I think you should take this call."

Mike was married to a medium named Irene. They had published a book about Abraham Lincoln's use of mediums during the Civil War that I was using in my workshops.

"Ok," I said. "Give me a second."

I turned off the shower, quickly toweled off the best I could, and walked over to the bathroom door. Connie opened it a little, handed me my cell phone and went back to her office. I set my towel down and brought the phone up to my still slightly wet ear.

"Hello Mike. How are you doing?"

"Ron, it's so great to hear your voice. Thank you for taking my call."

"It's my pleasure. What can I do for you?"

"I know you were friends with Irene, so I just wanted you to know that she passed away yesterday. We were relaxing by the pool, and just like that, she was gone. She suffered a massive heart attack," he said sadly.

"Mike, I'm so sorry."

"Yeah, I'm really going to miss her. But I know that you and Irene, because of the work you were doing, understand that physical death isn't the end. You know that life continues afterwards."

As Mike continued talking, I received a picture of Irene's face in my mind's eye. Then I began to realize that her spiritual presence was with me, and that she wanted to convey a message to Mike.

"Mike, Irene is here right now, and she wants to say something to you."

Mike and Irene had married late in life. And Irene started to explain what that had meant to her.

"Irene wants you to know how happy she was to be married to you. Before she met you, she had arrived at that age where some women think 'Nobody's going to want to marry me now. I'm too old.' She had resigned herself to the likelihood that she would probably spend the rest of her life alone. And then you came along! She is so grateful to have found you, even though it was later in life, and for the years that the two of you had together before she passed."

Mike was so happy to receive this message. It resonated with his feelings as well.

"You know, Ron," he said, "I can you tell you that I was well aware that Irene felt that way about me. Thank you so much for sharing that with me."

"You're welcome. Let me know if there's anything else I can do for you. All the best to you and your family."

"Thanks again, Ron. That really meant a lot to me."

"You're welcome."

After we ended the call, I lay my cell phone down on the sink, and started to finish drying off. Then it dawned on me that I had just given my first reading in the nude. I wondered, "Could Irene see me standing here naked while she was communicating with me?"

The short answer to that question is, I don't know, but my best guess is, I don't think so.

During the whole experience, the atmosphere surrounding the call was sacred. There was an aura of holiness about it. I forgot that I was naked, and Irene never said anything like, "For God's sake Ron, put your robe on!"

So, I really don't think she could see that I was naked.

It was a little startling to have Irene make her presence known so strongly out of the blue like that, but since she is a medium and is well acquainted with the phenomenon of spirit communication, it doesn't surprise me that she was able to get my attention even while I was standing in my bathroom still dripping from my morning shower.

13 - Growth After Death

I mentioned in the introduction that some of the things I learned through interacting with "dead people" caused me to question and ultimately discard many of the beliefs I had acquired while growing up. One of those had to do with what happened to people after they "died." In my youth I embraced a belief system that presented the afterlife as a static place; you lived your life on the earth, and then you were judged and arrived at a place that was more or less a final destination. You either went to heaven, hell, or purgatory. In the case of heaven and hell, your fate was settled for eternity. Only purgatory contained an opportunity for improving your situation. My understanding was that our actions on earth sealed our fate in the spirit world. There wasn't much one could do to change their situation once they made the transition to the other side. I also assumed that there was no further personal growth or learning in the spirit world.

The communications I have received from Josh and others that took place while I performed mediumistic readings challenged this mindset. For example, one can clearly see that Josh made tremendous progress in his spiritual growth between the time of the first letter we received from the medium in Texas and the second one.

Josh alludes to that growth in this brief excerpt of a message he gave through my friend David Hose. I was having a chat with David one day over the telephone when he unexpectedly began receiving communication from Josh. I grabbed a writing pad and jotted notes as fast as I could, but missed some of what he said:

November 15, 2003

I want to say Hi, Mom and Dad. I have been very close to both of you. I know Mom your emotions at this time. I want to say a few things about my process since coming here. I left my body and earth experience way behind. But not the family love since before my birth, instituted by God.

I am on the path to discover my true spiritual self.

I am learning a lot, growing a lot. I desire to reach out to others like me. Some guides knew my same darkness. I'm studying to take greater responsibility.

Stay close together, pray together, contact me directly, because you know me.

In a short time, Josh had progressed from a soul full of anxiety, remorse, and self-doubt to a person more at ease and hopeful about the future in his new-found life.

This phenomenon is even more evident here in his third letter:

Reading with Josh Pappalardo
May 30, 2004

Hi everyone, this is Josh.

It's good to be back with you through this communication. However, it is not as if I haven't been around to see you. I come to you often, very often. People will say that those who pass to this side must go on with their lives, and in a sense, should be forgotten. Nothing is further from the truth. This is the world of heart. We are meant to keep a natural and rich relationship flowing between us beyond the "seeming" separation of these two worlds (physical and spiritual). And so, this is what I intend to do.

I appreciate that you acknowledged my birthday. That really touched me. After all, I am still here. This is what I love about my family. Compared with most of the world, you are very progressive, enlightened. I am not saying you are perfect, but to me you're pretty close to that, and I love you.

I would like to share with you some of my adventures. I could chit-chat forever about this and that, but I want you to know substantially what I am doing on this side. I never waver from my responsibilities and commitments, you will be happy to know. I take everything very seriously. Maybe this is to make up for how I failed in the physical realm. These are lessons I need to learn. The education continues whether we are in the physical realm or on this side. I share with you all that I am doing because I want you to experience how alive I am. Please, don't dwell on my passing. This has been the destiny I chose. If I were still on the earth, I know that I would still be very miserable, in a mess of a life, and you would too, just watching me waste my life.

Here, my life is full and I can honestly say that I am happy and at peace with myself. I am involved with people. I grew up in a home of total involvement with others, but I resisted that. Maybe I felt that the involvement of my parents in the lives of others was at my expense. And it was, to some degree. But now I can see beyond that. Maybe there has to be a healthy balance and that was missing.

Here, I am totally involved with others. At first, I was involved with groups of young people who passed to this world in the same manner as me. It was like looking at myself over and over, and listening to many of the thoughts and crumpled ideas I had going in my mind over and over through the lives of these young people. On many levels I could confront and forgive myself for what I did. I could also reconcile my pain and anger and rebellion. I cried a lot together with other young people, and we raised *ourselves into realms of higher consciousness. We moved into spaces of freedom (from our thoughts, emotions, and regrets). Once we could move into higher realms of light and freedom, we could choose what to do. We don't have video games, TV, Nintendo and things like that here. Anyway, that is so superficial to what is real and alive here that we never desire it. Well, I did when I first came to this side and was still tied to the physical realm with my thoughts and emotions. But having moved to other realms of light totally frees us of the strings that tie us to stuff of the world.*

Life is so rich and bright and beautiful here. I have flown. I have flown and it is so amazing. We fly like birds here. No airplanes, no ultralights, just our arms outstretched, and free as birds! And so, this has been so amazing. I have visited realms of learning and of music and the arts. You know how I love music. This is a remarkable space to visit and study in. The music is of such fine quality that it lifts our spirits and brings us into total love. It expresses beauty, love, peace, and joy, all at the same time. And everyone just lights up with it, so we then can take the music to a higher level. This is how it goes; we get lighter and lighter until we are totally in harmony and love. I could live in this realm forever, but it has a purpose. That is to give nourishment to our souls so that we can impart these virtues to those who we reach out to when we return to our realm of work.

I have chosen to work with young people. This is where I feel comfortable. I work one-on-one with each person. It is not as a professional, but as one who has learned from experience. So, I have in my charge two or three young people at a time. Right now, I have Cynthia, Sherri and Margo. They have all passed in the very recent past (within weeks of earth time). They also chose to take their life. Margo is the youngest, only thirteen. I listen to them, give them energy and comfort. This doesn't affect me as it did when I just came here. I feel totally free of all that heaviness. And since I can visit the realm of music and the arts, I am able to give them this light. Here it is like receiving food and nourishment. If I try to describe what I do, I realize that it sounds like nothing. But that is because it is so difficult to put into words what transpires in the spiritual realms.

It is like trying to explain a beautiful deep dream in words. It just doesn't come out the same. And so, it is with my work here. I have chosen to be involved with others in their healing.

Mom and Dad, you may wonder what you can do to support me. I want to ask you to please pray to be guided to the parents or loved ones of others who have taken their lives or even who have died young. Offer them your support, comfort, and love. You are so privileged to understand so much in your hearts and so you have the ability to raise the consciousness of parents who are lost in their despair after their child or loved one died (especially if they took their own life). I know the depth of regret from taking one's life. And we are all well aware of that pain of our parents, siblings and loved ones. I know that you also accused yourselves for what happened. And some parents or siblings will even follow their child, sister, or brother to this side eventually because they couldn't get past this point. This is such a burden to us. I know that if you just put out the intention to be of support of other parents, or form a support group and put it out on the Internet, you will draw to you so many people who will be uplifted and reborn by coming in relationship with you. Start with just one person or family, and go from there.

From here we will try to connect the parents of the children I am working with to you. Just put it out into the universe and we will all work together. I know that you are doing something along these lines already, but I just want to encourage you to expand your work. Get the whole family involved. It will be your healing experience and will be your path of enlightenment!

I have one more thing to say to you. I love you so much. I come to you often and I know that you are aware of me when I'm in your presence. Please keep that door of communication open. I want you to be reassured that I am totally in a space of love and happiness. I didn't mention that I visit also other realms of learning. There are many things that I study. It is my desire to grow and to be a beacon of light to others. I study literature. I love to read. Does that surprise you! And so, I am growing, giving, and loving.

I reach out to you and my sister and brothers. I love you all so much and I give to you some of this beautiful light and love that I'm experiencing. Be open!
  All my love,
  Josh

14 - *Evidentiary* Mediumship

The evidence for survivability is overwhelming and increasing day by day. According to a 2011 Gallup Poll, it was estimated that three percent of Americans have had a Near Death Experience (NDE), which is over 9 million people![13] Many NDE experiencers report direct encounters with deceased family members, Angels, and even God.

One way that mediumship contributes to the proof of survivability is by providing material that is *evidentiary*. While practicing mediumship, I often receive symbols, images, words, and feelings that make no sense to me, but have profound meaning to the *sitter*. (Sitter is the term mediums use for a person who requests a reading. It simply comes from the fact that in order to receive a reading, a person visits a medium and sits in their presence. These days quite a few mediums, including myself, do most of their work over the telephone, but the term sitter has survived.)

---

[13] Charles Q. Choi. "Peace of Mind: Near-Death Experiences Now Found to Have Scientific Explanations." *Scientific American* 12 Sep. 2011. scientificamerican.com Web. 19 Jun. 2021.

For example, I recently did a reading for a middle-aged woman from Denmark. During the reading, another woman appeared in my mind's eye. I told my sitter that the feeling I got was that this woman was her deceased mother. (Knowing something by sensing it intuitively is called *clairsentience*.) I described her hair, full-bodied with a wave to it, and my sitter confirmed that her mother did indeed have hair like that. One could easily say that might have been a lucky guess, but then I could see clearly through clairvoyance that her mother was holding a bouquet of white daisies. I informed the sitter and she immediately replied, "Oh yes. White daisies were her favorite flowers." That is what we mean by *evidentiary mediumship*. There's no way I could have known that her deceased mother's favorite flowers were white daisies.

Another example took place when I did a reading for a woman who was an immigrant from Italy. I didn't see any image of a person, but I received through clairvoyance a scene of a garden trellis right next to the front door of a house. I could also see that there were red roses growing on the trellis. When I described the scene to the sitter, she replied that her mother had such a trellis with roses on it growing at the front door of her house in Italy. From this image we were able to deduce that it was her mother who was trying to communicate in the reading.

Spirits will often communicate information to me that makes it easy for the sitter to identify who they are. Again, the information is meaningless to me, but the sitter is aware of what the information represents.

When the phenomena of Modern Spiritualism broke out in force in 1848 the vast quantity of evidentiary mediumship that was produced made it difficult for skeptics to deny the reality of survivability. Skeptics tried to explain it away by saying that mediums were not establishing communication with spirits of the deceased on the other side, but actually drawing the information out of the brains of the sitters through some form of telepathy. They were willing to concede the reality of *Extra Sensory Perception* (ESP), but not the existence of life after death and a spirit world.

An additional phenomenon then began to be noticed that made it impossible for this argument to hold up. It is the phenomenon of spirits revealing information that is unknown to the sitter at the time of the reading but becomes confirmed to the sitter after the reading is over. The best way for me to explain it is to give a couple of examples:

In September of 2011, Connie and I traveled to the Washington, DC area for a book signing. After speaking at the event, I agreed to perform a *gallery reading*. A gallery reading is a demonstration of mediumship done in front of a group of people, as opposed to an individual sitter. I don't believe there were more than twenty people present, but I remember vividly being drawn to a particular woman sitting in the audience. Her name was Wendy Herstein. Standing just to the right of where Wendy was sitting, I could see a female spirit. The woman bore a striking resemblance to Wendy; they could have been sisters or even fraternal twins. She was wearing clothes that seemed to be about one-hundred years old. Through clairsentience, I could tell that this woman was Irish.

"Do you have Irish ancestry?" I asked Wendy.

"I don't think so," she said. "My people were mostly German."

"Well, I see an Irish lady standing next to you, and she looks a lot like you." Then I surprised myself by saying something that just came to me from out of the blue. "You ought to check some old family photo albums and see what you might find," I said.

In November, we returned to the area to conduct a one-day workshop. As I was standing at the front of the meeting room preparing to start the program, a woman came walking up the center aisle towards me with great excitement. It was Wendy. My guess was since she had enjoyed the book signing so much, she decided to come to the workshop. In her hands she was carrying two photographs.

"I want to show you something," she said, beaming from ear to ear, and held up the photographs. One was in color; the other in black and white.

"The color photo is me," she said, "when I was in my twenties. The other one is my Irish great-grandmother, who was also in her twenties when it was taken."

When I compared the two photos, they seemed to be of the same person. The resemblance was remarkable. The only difference I could see was that the woman in the black and white photo was dressed in clothes from a much earlier time period, maybe the late nineteenth or early twentieth century, while the color photo of Wendy revealed a young woman dressed in the style of the late 1980s.

The extraordinary factor of this episode is that it would have been impossible for me to extract the information about Wendy's Irish great-grandmother out of her brain through mental telepathy because *Wendy herself didn't know she had an Irish great-grandmother!*

The second example comes from a reading I did in 2020. A younger woman, perhaps in her thirties, had recently lost her sister, and wanted to see if I could make contact with her in the spiritual world. During the reading, I was able to sense the presence of the ascended sister, and to convey some of her thoughts and feelings which seemed to be well received by her earthly sister. Towards the end of the reading, the sitter asked me "Can you give me something that can prove to me that you're definitely communicating with my sister?"

I asked her to give me a couple of minutes of silence to really focus my attention on her sister and see if I could get anything that would be more evidentiary. I closed my eyes, and I received the image of a Christian cross. It was not just some generic cross; it was clearly a Roman Catholic cross. A Protestant cross is usually a simple plain cross with nothing else depicted on it, but on a Roman Catholic cross the figure of Jesus is usually depicted, crucified on the cross.

I asked the young woman, "Are you Catholic?"

"No," she replied.

"Are any members of your family Catholic?"

"I don't know. I don't think so," she said.

"Well, I don't know what to tell you. I'm seeing the image of a cross, but it's very clearly a Roman Catholic cross. I can see the figure of Jesus hanging on this cross. Another strange thing about this cross is that it is part of a necklace, but the necklace is not made of metal. I've seen these things before and they're usually hanging on a gold or silver chain. This cross is hung from some soft material, like cloth or a ribbon of some kind."

As in Wendy's case, I don't know why I said what I said next, but it was a suggestion that just came from out of the blue. "You might want to ask your mom about this cross."

A few days later, I received an email from this young woman. She had followed my advice and spoken to her mother. It turns out that her mother had been given this cross by her brother just before her sister's funeral. He requested that it be put in the coffin, so she placed it there and rested her daughter's hands on top of it.

Along with the email, my sitter attached a photograph of the cross. To my delight, it was indeed a Roman Catholic cross, a crucifix, with the body of Jesus affixed to it. Even more evidentiary, the necklace was not made of a metal chain. It was some type of softer material; it looked like a narrow cord of leather to me. Both the mother and the sister were astonished at the accuracy of the description, and that it was a direct part of the funeral service, the last day they would see their loved one's face.

Again, it would have been impossible for me to extract this information out of the mind of my sitter because she had no knowledge of the existence of this cross until she asked her mom about it.

What I find even more interesting is that the spirits employ this technique often. I've experienced a pattern where spirits will reveal information that the sitter is not aware of until further research, instead of just revealing information that the sitter is already aware of. I'm just guessing, but I think they do this on purpose to enhance the power and effectiveness of spirit communication. By making it so dramatic, spirits make a much stronger impression on everyone involved, adding credibility to the phenomenon. That's important, because we are talking about proof that their loved ones still exist on the "other side." People will sometimes have an experience with a medium and in that moment they are convinced and deeply moved in their hearts, only to allow doubts to creep in afterwards. In cases like the two I described above the experience is much less likely to be doubted later.

Evidentiary Mediumship

After I received an image of a cross on a necklace during a reading, my client, who had no prior knowledge of its existence, spoke to her mother, who sent her this image. The image confirmed, in detail, what I had received clairvoyantly.

15 - Work Occupations of the Dead

Josh's personal growth in the spiritual world was rapid and a source of great comfort and inspiration to me. In less than a year, he went from being like a patient in a rehabilitation facility to finding a "job" ministering comfort and healing to those who were new arrivals in the spirit world.

In the book *Life in the World Unseen* the spirit of Monsignor Robert Hugh Benson explains in more detail the process of finding a work occupation in the spirit world. Monsignor Benson tells us that when spirits have settled into their new life in the spirit world, they "will soon find something which attracts their attention and draws their interest." Spirits have a wide variety of occupations to choose from:

> *The spirit world is not only a land of equal opportunity for every soul, but the opportunities are upon so vast a scale that no person still incarnate can have the least conception of its magnitude. Opportunities for what? – It will be asked. Opportunities for good, useful, interesting work.*

... the spirit world is not a land of idleness, not a land where its inhabitants spend the whole of their lives in a super-ecstatic atmosphere of religious exercises, formally offering up 'prayer and praise' to the Great Throne in a never ceasing flow. There is an uninterrupted flow, most certainly, but it comes about in a very different way. It surges up from the hearts of us all, who are happy to be here, and thankful withal.

...behind the earth world's occupations is the ever driving necessity of earning a living, of providing the physical body with food and drink, clothing and a habitation of some sort ... these last four considerations have no existence whatever with us here. Food and drink we never need; the clothing and the habitation we have provided for ourselves by our lives upon earth. As our lives have been on earth, so will our clothing and our domicile be when we come to spirit lands. We have, as you see, no physical necessity to work, but we do have a mental necessity to work, and it is because of the latter that all work is a pleasure with us here.

Imagine yourself in a world where no one works for a living, but where everyone works for the sheer joy of doing something that will be of service to others. ...You will begin to understand something of the life in spirit lands. [14]

One form of work which is widely engaged in is gardening:

Scores of people upon the earth plane love gardens and gardening. Some have engaged in the latter as their calling, and enjoyed doing it. What better than to

---

[14] Anthony Borgia. *Life in the World Unseen.* Midway, Utah: M.A.P. Inc. 1993. pp. 163-164

continue with their work here in the spirit world, unrestrained by physical exigencies, free and unhampered, and with the inexhaustible resources of the spirit world at their command?

...They can – and do – stop whenever they wish. And there is no one to exert his will upon them. And what is the result? Happiness for themselves, because by creating a beautiful work of horticultural art they have added more beauty to an already beautiful realm, and in doing so they have brought happiness to others. So their task goes on, altering, rearranging, planning, beautifying, building anew, and ever acquiring skill and still greater skill. Thus they continue until such time as they wish to change their work, or until their spiritual progression carries them on to fresh fields of endeavor in other realms. [15]

Other occupations involve construction:

Now let us go into the hall of music, and see what work we can find there. Someone, of course, had to plan, and others to build, the Hall itself. ... In all major building operations the method followed is the same, but the methods of the spirit will have to be learned, and the work of the architects and builders, with their various expert assistance, is among some of the most important in the spirit world. As all descriptions of employment are open to anyone who has the taste for such work, that of the architect and builder is, likewise, free to all who express a preference for continuing their earthly occupation, or who wish to turn to something new. The wish to do so is really all that is required, although, naturally, an aptitude is a great help. But it is very

---

[15] Ibid. pp. 165

surprising how quickly efficiency is gained by the stimulus of desire. The 'wish to do' becomes translated into the 'ability to do' in a very short time. Keen interest and predilection for the work are all that are asked. [16]

Many are drawn to music:

Inside the hall of music we find libraries of music, where students are busy at their studies, and pupils with their musician teachers. Most of the people whom we meet thus are learning to be practical musicians; that is, they are learning to play one or more instruments. And someone has to provide them with the necessary instruments. The hall of music does that, but somebody must create them for the hall of music. And so the instrument makers of the earth plane find themselves at home in their craft if they wish to continue with it in the spirit world. [17]

In Phillip Burley's 2018 book *Voices of Love from the Light*, the spirit of Albert Einstein reveals many more intimate details about the work that goes on in the spirit world:

I work in a lab. In your wildest imaginings, you could not comprehend what that means because, rather than mixing chemicals for various experiments, we work with light and energy. We still try things out, but everything is known. Information is filtered to us from higher consciousness or higher masters. They deliver answers through flashing insights into our awareness, showing us, for example, where one thing could be

---

[16] Anthony Borgia. Life in the World Unseen. Midway, Utah: M.A.P. Inc. 1993. p.165
[17] Ibid. p. 165-166

combined well with another. We also have our own God consciousness, and we can tap into that source, or universal energy, so we do not have to struggle to find answers.

The greatest struggle comes in trying to bring inventions to earth. Television is a prime example. Many scientists gathered in the spirit world to work on the idea of television before it came to the earth plane, but it already existed in the mind of God. Television existed side by side with the dinosaur, if you understand what I am saying. It was just a matter of time to create the earthly environment to bring forth everything, dinosaurs first and television later. (Laughter) Some of the work happened in Russia and other places, but in the western world, Filo T. Farnsworth was the primary target of efforts by the spirit world to pass ideas to earth about television. Creating a device that could pick up energy waves and translate them into pictures on a tube was extremely complicated and took a lot of thought, but Filo T. Farnsworth was impressed by the spirit world in such a way that he could pick up the ideas. He had a brilliance or genius about him when he came to the earth plane. You might say Mr. Farnsworth was born to invent the television. [18]

There are other occupations that don't involve creating anything. These are occupations that are focused on serving others, such as the work Joshua has chosen to do, ministering to the needs of suicides after they arrive in the spirit world. One occupation that appeals to me personally is the practice of visiting lower vibration spiritual realms for the purpose of ministering to those who are

---

[18] Philip Burley. *Voices of Love from the Light.* Phoenix, Arizona: Mastery Press. 2018. pp.225-226

dwelling there. I can see myself doing this when I cross over to the other side.

This activity is described in the book *Letters from Summerland* by Marion Young Starnes. The book contains a large selection of communications Starnes has had with the spirit of her recently-deceased husband, James, who describes his work visiting a realm he refers to as the "Gray" area or zone:

> *Marian: . . . what lies ahead for you in your new life? What is your work or duties over there?*
>
> *James: Service, always service. That is the motto for everyone here. New arrivals quickly pick up the joy of being able to help others. Everyone works, if you can really call it such, to get balanced and energetically fit, in order to play a productive role . . .*
>
> *Marian: Is the service to those still embodied in human form, or is it just in your world or other parts of the spirit realm? What do you do?*
>
> *James: It is both . . . Some, like myself, have been given permission to work in the Gray area. That is where I go to talk to Troy, Grady and Brad. As they learn, and want to move upward, they will be able to leave there for a higher plane. Love is the only way, so I talk to them a lot about forgiveness and love. I have chosen this work which hardly seems like work at all. It is so deeply rewarding for me personally.*
>
> *My other "mission" is to work with you to try to teach that there is no death, only Life ever expanding, changing. Again, I volunteered to do this. There aren't any "bosses." Everyone just seems to know what needs to be done and they do it.* [19]

---

[19] Marion Young Starnes. *Letters from Summerland.* Cedar Mountain, North Carolina: Terra Nova Publishing. 1996. p.44

The "Gray" area James describes reminds me of the Roman Catholic concept of purgatory. The point I want to emphasize here is that existence in the spirit world is not static; there is lots of movement. Even though a spirit might spend many years dwelling in a place that some might describe as a "hell," there is no such thing as an eternal state of damnation. Even the most troubled person can ascend into higher and higher realms over time.

16 - Josh Comforts His Mom

Connie's path to healing was a more painful and gradual process than mine and took years to fully complete. She suffered with feelings of guilt and remorse for his passing, and I think she felt a sense of loss on a deeper level than I did. After all, Josh was formed in and came forth from within her. He was literally a part of her physical body. I think being his biological mother created a unique closeness and intimacy that I could never have experienced.

About a year after the letter in which Josh describes his work with young suicides, we received another letter that was specifically addressed to Connie. She had just concluded a telephone call with the medium from Texas in which she poured out her heart about how she was still deeply grieving and missing him terribly.

After they ended the call, the medium, Ms. G, unexpectedly felt Josh's presence and received this message:

May 29, 2005

Mom, I saw that Ms. G was talking with you this morning and I had to come. I am longing so much to speak to you because I see that you are sad. *If you could see the brilliance of this world that I live in, experience the wholeness that is, you would be so comforted and you would be so happy, not just because you would know that I am fine, but because you would be so transformed by the beauty and wonder of this world of spirit. You would experience your own brilliance and beauty!*

You call my name often and I want you to know that every single time you hold my name in your breath, I come to you Mom. I come and stand there beside you. You are sad only because you "think" that we are apart. You miss me only because you do not "feel" me right there with you. Do you understand that you just have to grasp this reality of the world of spirit and instantly you will find yourself in what is true? Everything else is just made-up Mom. You are suffering because you live in a world of make believe, a world that has been created by human consciousness, that has little to do with what is real.

I did not know this myself. This is why I was so lost. I think that you and I were lost together, Mom. At times I see you in the same space (of thinking) that I was in and I can see that it is so futile. It takes you nowhere, just to misery. Then when I came to this side, I discovered that we had it all wrong. But I was already on this side and I already had committed this grave error of tearing myself from the physical.

The point is Mom that you don't have to do this. The anguish that it brings up in one is unbearable. I have gone past that point and I'm happy to say that I do not struggle with this. I do work with young people every moment of my life who are going through this, and I can tell you that this is not easy.

I was so blessed to have made a very quick transition and to have moved into a higher consciousness. And so, I could leave the old concepts of what is life behind and embrace the world of being, just being one with God, the universe, everyone and everything that is alive. But many young people that I work with are so stuck in the past. They cannot forgive and so they relive the past over and over. We try to reach them in many ways, and we never give up. I love them so much, Mom. Can you believe it, I love? And it is this love that eventually draws them out of their pain.

I tell you this so that you are comforted, so that you can have hope and that you can realize that the moment you are ready to move out of your grief and despair over my passing, there will be those who will help you along. This is how it is here, too. And one more thing. When you dwell on the sadness, then you are going somewhere else than where I am. Then you feel further from me and it's understandable. I just am in a beautiful space of love and warmth, of endless beauty. I want to hold your hand and bring you into the space of wonder so that you will be free, Mom. Don't resist. Let go of the past. You have to embrace the moment. The past is dead.

And so, I leave you with this song:

I walk in the rain by your side,
I sing you a song of the love we share
I'll do anything
To help you understand
I love you more than
Anybody can.

I love you Mom. Josh.

17 - Josh's New Job

After a few more years, Josh began to communicate that the focus of his work had shifted. Instead of just working with the spirits of those who had crossed over due to suicide, helping them to heal, his attention shifted back to the earth plane. He began working with kindred spirits—no pun intended—who also had a special concern for those who were struggling with suicide. He called them a special "Task Force."

Their mission was to prevent suicides from taking place. They would do this by using their spiritual influence to help those struggling with anxiety and depression. While they were working from the spirit side, they also needed to partner with people still alive on the earth plane. Josh made it clear to me—and with a sense of humor—that whether I liked it or not I was a part of his "Task Force."

It became apparent to me that a central part of my role would be to write a book telling Josh's story and the lessons learned from it. Through a medium named Sherry Lassiter, he said that writing the book would open a lot of doors so I could reach more people.

He said I would be invited to speak in various places; these things he predicted came to pass.

After I finished my first draft of the book, I sent it to the medium in Texas for her to look over. Just after she finished composing an email to me in which she shared her impressions of the draft, Josh unexpectedly came to her and gave this communication:

January 11, 2009

Hi Ms. G, this is Josh. I had to come and talk to you today because I saw that you read my story and you have been writing to my dad. Thank you for reading my story, and for taking the time to express your sentiments to my dad. He poured so much into this book. People in general don't know that there is no divide between the physical and the spiritual worlds. They get to death and then everything is "the end." There is no room in their minds to conceive of what is beyond physical existence, even if they believe in life after death. And so, the word that is used is "death," the end, finished. But there is so much more! Life has meaning and it is eternal.

My Dad would be happy to hear that I am aware of the book, and that I have peeked into it . . . and even helped to write it. You have to tell him this. My parents will want to know what I am doing now and how I am. I am fine, I am working always, studying, growing and being a participant in "life" which I was not in the physical world.

Transitioning to the spiritual world affords us the opportunity to blend back into the source of all that is, to lose ourselves and the particular identities we took on while on the earth and become one with the Source. We move from this tiny sense of insignificant self to a feeling of wholeness and completeness that is difficult to describe. We are one heartbeat, one breath, one essence together with all that is — the wind, music, others . . . spirit. My parents like to look at photos of me as a child and remember what life was like with me. The truth is that what they are trying to grasp is the "feeling" of Josh, and that feeling of Josh is in them because I am in them. You look puzzled Ms. G. I know it's hard to conceive of what I am trying to convey, but just say it this way. My Mom is an artist. They get it.

And so, that self-absorption that one finds so difficult to shake even upon transitioning to this side, is gone. My sense of Josh as I lived on the earth is faded and all I know is that I am a part of my parents lives, my family and friends. I matter to them, and they matter to me. I impacted the lives of others — in good ways and I am proud of that. I have let go of that which was painful and difficult to comprehend about my life existence, so I cannot tell you much of that. It is not in my space.

Please tell my dad that I love him and that I am proud of his commitment to writing this book. My mother has dealt with my passing also through her own creativity and she is the light of my life! Both of my parents have done so much to heal my heart, which has also healed theirs. I think that we all believe that we accomplish what we came to the earth to accomplish in our lifetime. But that is not necessarily the case. We continue to grow in spirit. And when we are blessed with parents such as mine, then we are able to grow so much. Life has meaning. This has been God's grace upon me – the love and devotion of my parents for me, even after I have passed to the spiritual world.

Who could ask for more?

Mom, Dad . . . I love you.

Josh

18 - Being Part of Josh's Team

Joshua had a great sense of humor in life, and he carried that with him into the spiritual world. One amusing as well as profound story took place during one of the speaking tours Connie and I conducted for students at colleges. We were spending a lot of time in Pennsylvania, speaking about preventing suicide at various campuses that are part of the Pennsylvania State University system. We were driving back home to North Carolina, traveling along a rural highway somewhere between Reading and Gettysburg. One of the things Connie and I enjoy the most about traveling is getting off the Interstate highways. We can drive slower through the countryside, visiting the people in the small towns along the way.

The sun had just gone down, and as the twilight slowly turned to night, we were looking for a place to have dinner. I saw a billboard for something like a "Carriage House Restaurant," and started heading in what I thought was the right direction. But that was not meant to be. I was never able to find the Carriage House restaurant, but instead stumbled onto a quaint town square, with a charming little restaurant calling to us from one corner. Connie and

I decided it would do just fine and pulled into one of the open parking spaces on the street.

We were seated by a friendly waitress, and at some point, while making small talk she asked us what had brought us into town. When I explained to her the work we were doing, and that I was a medium, her eyes widened with eager interest.

It turned out that she was intrigued by the subject of spirit communication, and if I remember correctly, had a close connection with a teenage boy who was struggling with depression. I got the impression that she might have been concerned about the possibility of suicide as well.

When she heard about the book I had written, *Reconciled by the Light: The After-Death Letters from a Teen Suicide* she asked if I had an extra copy that she could buy from us that night. I wolfed down my meal faster than Connie, so while she was finishing up, I went out to the car to get the book. The waitress purchased it with her tip money, and when we finished our meal Connie and I walked up to the cash register to settle our bill. As the waitress was processing our payment her eyes grew wide again and she said, "Joshua is here right now. I can feel him."

"What do you feel?" I asked.

"So much love!" She appeared deeply moved.

We said our goodbyes and promised to stay in touch. Then we walked out to the car to resume are homeward journey. The charming little town faded in my rear-view mirror, and a couple of miles into the countryside I received a surprising remark from Connie.

"Poochie-Man!" she exclaimed, using her endearing nickname for me.

"What?" I said, intrigued.

"Focus on Josh for a minute and tell me if you see anything!"

Even without closing my eyes, while focusing my attention on Joshua I could see his face in my mind's eye. There was one unusual additional detail. He was holding his left arm straight up with his hand next to his face, and slightly moving his palm. It reminded me of the way the Queen ceremonially waves to the crowds at Buckingham Palace.

"I can see his face," I said, "and he's holding his hand up like this, like he's waving to me." I made the gesture to Connie that I saw in my mind's eye. She just laughed.

"No, he's not waving to you. He wants to give you a 'high-five,'" she said. "He just gave me a high-five. You know, it's like he's saying, 'We're all part of the same team!'"

Astonished, I came to the conclusion that the whole encounter with the waitress had been orchestrated by Joshua. I thought about the fact that I got the impulse to look for a restaurant just a moment before I saw the billboard with the Carriage House sign. Then about how I changed directions to drive down the road that I thought would take me there. Then, I remembered how surprised I was when after a couple of miles, I saw no sign of the Carriage House and instead was attracted to the little restaurant on the corner of the quaint town square.

Then we were served by a waitress who coincidentally had an unusual interest in the subject of our work and who spontaneously decided to buy a copy of my book. The icing on the cake was when I recalled how Joshua made his presence felt at the cash register, and how the energy of his love moved the waitress to the core of her heart.

Even though I felt the sense of Joshua's playful sense of humor, that feeling was overshadowed by a deeper, more profound understanding of the meaningful—perhaps even sacred—nature of the work the three of us were doing together. I realized that without the efforts of those in heaven and willing partners on the earth, Divine intentions can go unfulfilled.

"Wow!" I thought. "We really are all part of the same team."

The first time Connie and I were both able to "see" Joshua at the same time happened in February of 2012. I had been invited to give a Suicide Prevention talk at a church in Raleigh. It was a fundamentalist Christian church and had a traditional Biblical doctrine regarding life after death. In a nutshell, this church taught that when someone died, they were buried "six feet under" and would remain there "asleep in Christ" until the return of Jesus on Resurrection Day. Then the physical bodies of the dead would rise out of their graves and come back to life.

I was a little nervous about what might happen if the subject of spirit communication came up. The Suicide Prevention part of my program was well-received, and then came the question and answer session. That went well, too, until a woman asked me a question about handling grief.

"How did you deal with the sadness that came from losing your son?" she asked.

"Well," I answered, "I believe in the 'gift of prophecy,' so I sought to get communication from my son after he died. By doing that, I was comforted by the knowledge that he was still around, and that he was okay."

That's all I said about spirit communication, but that was plenty. The pastor became very agitated, and after I fielded a couple more questions, he felt compelled to come up and try to undo the damage I had done to his dogma.

He took the microphone from me, and I sat down. He reminded the congregation that dead people were sleeping in their graves, so that it wasn't possible to get messages from them. He also warned them, with particular emphasis to the young people, that Satan was a tricky fellow, and they would be wise to stay to the tried-and-true path of fundamentalist Christianity. It seems to me that the pastor was essentially telling the group that I was an instrument of the Devil. I didn't get upset or angry, but just retired from the fight with a sigh.

To my surprise, he wasn't even happy with my suggestion that the best way to avoid suicidal thinking was to make a strong personal relationship with God. I had told the young people in particular that it was okay to say anything to God in prayer—to be honest about their feelings with him even if they were angry or upset.

I had said, "Prayer should be like a baby crying for its mother's milk."

The pastor didn't like that either.

Connie and I were sitting right in front of him in the first pew. While I found it amusing to watch the pastor flailing around spewing fear of damnation, I was really saddened by the thought that this fearfulness might wind up blocking people from opening their hearts to a direct experience with God. In my view, if our basic conception of God is that he is an angry sovereign ready to punish us miserable sinners any time we get out of line, this can block us from a genuine encounter of God's love.

It has been my experience, confirmed by numerous mystical experiences, that God is a loving parent eager to embrace us and honestly not very interested in judgment and "Hell-fire." So, it was with a feeling of disappointment that Connie and I left the church and climbed into our trusty Dodge van for the trip home. Driving down the interstate, I commented to Connie how sad it was that some members of the church were so closed to receiving any new information that might contradict their doctrine.

Immediately, I saw Joshua through clairvoyance. He was sitting in the back seat, head tilted down slightly, and shaking it back and forth. Through clairaudience, I heard him say "Those people, those people!" with an air of not exactly frustration in his voice, but more like bemusement and sadness at their closed-mindedness.

To my surprise, Connie said, "Joshua's in the back seat!"

"You see him, too?" I asked.

"Yeah," she replied. "He's shaking his head, 'No.'"

I was astonished. "I saw him shaking his head back and forth, too, but I heard him saying 'Those people, those people.' I think he's disappointed that they weren't more open-minded."

"Yeah, I think so, too," she said.

We were both amazed. While both Connie and I have had numerous separate spiritual encounters with Joshua, that time we both perceived his presence and location simultaneously.

19 - Kailee's Story

In addition to speaking engagements, I developed a two-day workshop to teach some of the things I had learned about the spiritual life. I had come to the conclusion that a major reason young people in particular turn to suicide was because of something psychiatrist Viktor Frankl called an *existential vacuum*. It seemed apparent to me that a large percentage of American young people had a very weak sense of identity, and had a hard time finding meaning in life. I discovered that introducing them to the spiritual side of reality contributed greatly to their sense of well-being. In many cases it was life-transformative. One of the young people whose life was dramatically improved is a young lady named Kailee Earle. She was sixteen-years-old at the time. I gave her the pseudonym "Kristen" in the excerpt below from my book *Reconciled by the Light, Book II,* but she has since given me permission to use her real name.

One of the techniques I use in my workshops is a guided meditation I call the *Sun Meditation.* I begin by asking the participants to imagine that they are sitting in a chair on the beach on a bright sunny day. There comes a point during the workshop where the spiritual atmosphere becomes heightened, and that's when I introduce the meditation. In the session that Kailee participated in, my spiritual sight opened up and I saw something I had never seen before. I was standing in front of the room guiding about a dozen people through the meditation exercise. As I looked at their faces, I saw what looked like little gentle tornadoes of energy spiraling in front of some of them. The tornadoes were cone-shaped and long, like a trumpet or the megaphones cheerleaders use:

Kristen (not her real name) was sitting all the way in the back, off to my right. When I looked over at her, I was taken aback. In front of her face there was also a rotating vortex, but it wasn't the size of a trumpet; it was the size of a tuba! This thing was so huge it was as if she was completely immersed in spiritual energy. I knew that something amazing was going on with her, and I was dying to know what it was.

When the meditation finished, I stood up and returned to the front of the room.

"I could tell that you guys had some kind of spiritual experience," I said gesturing to the ones I saw the little tornadoes in front of, "and Kristen, you had a lot of stuff going on, didn't you?"

All Kristen could do was nod her head. I could see that her face was drenched in tears. She was still gently sobbing.

I asked each person if they wanted to share what had happened to them during the meditation. Just as my vision had indicated, the two participants that didn't have the vortexes in front of their faces said that while they enjoyed the meditation because it made them feel relaxed, they didn't have any experience out of the ordinary. One of them said her mind kept wandering, thinking about other things and distracting her from getting deeper into the meditation. This is a common challenge for beginners.

The ones that had the little tornadoes in front of them did have spiritual experiences. One woman choked up as she described a visitation she received from her deceased husband. Another had a deep realization about a particular question she had regarding her spiritual life path . . .

Finally, I asked Kristen if she would like to share something. She was still crying a little bit, even though a few minutes had passed since the meditation ended. I'm so grateful for her willingness to share her experience because I think it can be beneficial to a lot of people.

"After I got relaxed into my chair on the beach, I looked down the beach to my left, and I saw Joshua . . . down there," Kristen said. "So, I jumped out of my chair, ran down the beach as fast as I could, and tackle-hugged him. It was so great to feel his embrace. I just stayed there and talked with him. I told him how grateful I was to him for being my friend and for all he had done to help me.

"He just held me for a moment and then he spoke to me. He told me 'Actually, Kristen, you really shouldn't be thanking me. There's someone else who is really the one who helped you the most, and I'd like to introduce you to him.' Then he pointed to his left. When I looked over there, there was this bright white light. It was coming from the person standing next to Josh. As I looked to see who it was, I knew right away that it was God.

"I felt kind of nervous; I mean, this was God! So, I told him I was sorry—sorry because I felt I had been kind of ignoring him and didn't have a very good relationship with him.

"Then he said 'No, I'm sorry. I'm sorry that you have had such a difficult childhood. I'm sorry for what you have had to go through; it was never my intention that it should be like that.' Then he just hugged me, and I really started to cry then. I could actually feel him holding me. The feeling is just impossible to describe. I felt so accepted and loved—so loved! I didn't want it to end.

"Then he said, 'I've placed certain people in your life to help you. Joshua is one of them, but there are others on earth also. They are there just for you, because I love you so much! I am here for you also, whenever you call out for me! I also want to encourage you. You have so much love inside your heart, I hope you will share it with others—give it out. If you do this, it will be very good for you.'" [20]

A couple of weeks after her experience, I asked Kailee if anything in her life had changed as a result. She replied with just one word, "Tons." I asked her for a specific example. She thought for a moment, and then replied that before her prophetic experience, if she encountered a male student at her high school who was wearing what she described as a "ridiculous" shirt, she would usually make some kind of snarky remark or otherwise ridicule him. "I never do that kind of thing anymore," she said soberly.

Kailee's direct experience with God, which was accentuated by an overwhelmingly powerful communication from God of how much he loved her personally, of how precious she was to him, shifted her heart in such a way that it made it impossible for her to bully a fellow student anymore who she now identifies with as a spiritual brother of their common Heavenly Parent.

---

[20] Ron Pappalardo. *Reconciled by the Light book 2: Spirit Messages from a Teen Suicide: Adventures of a Psychic Medium.* Charleston: CreateSpace books. 2013. p. 31-32.

20 - Joshua Helps Create the Book

Even though the book, *Reconciled by the Light: The After-Death Letters from a Teen Suicide* opened many doors, it was no easy task to bring it to fruition. I was fortunate that while I was working on the book here on the earth plane, Joshua and others were helping to produce the book from the spirit side. At various points in the process, Joshua made his presence known, giving guidance and encouragement for its completion. In one message through a medium, Joshua said that there was a company that would be willing to publish the book, so I was moving forward in that direction. Months later, Joshua gave me a slightly different message directly through my own mediumship:

July 11, 2009

I'm happy with what you've been writing. This is really important content. I've been with you, as you have sensed, because I'm excited about what you've been doing. Don't let my prediction of September (for publisher to appear) influence you. If you feel strongly to self-publish, go for it!

That was just one possibility out there, but nothing's etched in stone. Don't worry about the job situation and money. Just focus on what you feel needs to be done. I am with you. You feel me right now (as you're writing this). There is a lot of support for this project in high places.

Also, it's okay to be patient. I know you're in a big hurry, but you needn't be. In one sense, there's plenty of time. While on the other hand, I feel/know your sense of urgency, and that's not a bad thing.

Josh

I had been trying to find a publisher for the book for over a year. Even though there was some interest, the changes requested from the publisher were of such a nature that they would have greatly delayed publication of the book. A further delay was my tendency to want the book to be as perfect as possible. Joshua communicated that it was not necessary to create a "perfect" book. He made me realize that the attempt to perfect it can become an endless process, delaying things unnecessarily. As a result of these messages, I made a firm decision to go ahead right away and self-publish the book. I'm really glad I decided to do that because speaking and workshop opportunities immediately opened up once I had a physical copy of the book in hand.

21 - Defeating Suicide

I've always had a special place in my heart for the Russian people, ever since I learned about their tragic history. It is a nation that produced some of my favorite sacred music, such as Tchaikovsky's *Hymn of the Cherubim* and some of the world's most beautiful art, poetry, and literature. I was spellbound by the movie adaptation of Boris Pasternak's *Doctor Zhivago* with its dreamlike imagery of the Russian countryside.

In 1917, Russia fell into the darkness of Soviet Communism. Its spiritual light was extinguished as churches and monasteries were confiscated by the state, and its official ideology became atheistic and materialistic. When I was a missionary there in the winter of 1990-1991, the spiritual atmosphere could be described in just three words: gray, dull, and lifeless. It was so sad to walk along the streets of Moscow where people avoided eye contact. I experienced trying to get a meal at a restaurant near the college I was staying at only to see the long line, including myself and many students, waved away by the workers when they ran out of food.

Yet, even before I left Russia, there were already signs of a spiritual springtime coming to life, like crocus flowers breaking through the soil even when there is still snow on the ground. There was a donation box in Red Square where ordinary citizens were giving money to reconstruct one of the great cathedrals that had been torn down by the communists. I was one of those who celebrated the collapse of the Soviet state later that year.

The demise of the Soviet Union opened up an opportunity for religious groups to become active. Many young Russians heard about God, who they referred to as "the God," for the first time. One of them was a young woman in her early twenties who, in order to protect her privacy, we will refer to as Katia. She was from Saratov, a city on the Volga River. It is located just a couple of hours' drive north of the site of one of the deadliest episodes of World War II, the Battle of Stalingrad, a bloodbath that lasted for more than five months.

Katia met a missionary, had a conversion experience, and became a believer. Her newfound faith presented an unexpected opportunity to emigrate to the United States. When I met her, she was living as a traditional housewife with her Russian husband and two young children in the Hudson Valley of upstate New York.

She reached out to me because she had read a copy of my first book *Reconciled by the Light: The After-Death Letters from a Teen Suicide.* During a lengthy telephone conversation, she explained that at first her sojourn into America had gone well. She was full of hope and excitement to be living in the "land of the free." Now that a few years had gone by, she found herself living frugally in a tiny apartment with her family, with little privacy, and losing hope of finding an improvement in her living situation. To make matters worse, her mother-in-law was living with them, criticizing her incessantly for her inability to be a perfect wife and mother. She had fallen into a deep depression, and confessed that she was entertaining suicidal thoughts.

In the several years since Josh's suicide, Connie and I had become amateur experts on the subject, reading everything we could get our hands on and speaking to people in support groups and others who had been touched by the tragedy. I knew that it was a very serious situation if a person contemplating suicide had progressed to the point where they had a plan of how they would take their lives.

"Katia," I asked as gently as I could. "If you decided to end your life, have you thought about how you would do it?"

Without hesitation Katia replied, "Oh, yes! It would be so easy just to crash my car into one of the large trees on the side of the road in my town."

For me, that was a red flag. I tried to think about what I could do to help this woman who was five hundred miles away from me at the time. Coincidentally, I was scheduled to hold a workshop in my home that weekend. These workshops were in many ways a follow up to my book. We would be spending a lot of time talking about suicide and ways to prevent it. I found myself wishing that we could hold it in Katia's town instead. I knew it was a long shot, but I told Katia about the workshop, and said that I regretted that it was being held in North Carolina because I was certain it would be very helpful to her. Katia's response was that she would see if it was possible for her to come down from New York.

To my amazement, in a very short time Katia came to an agreement with her husband that she would take time off from her job and arranged to take the Amtrak train down in time to attend the workshop. When Connie and I picked her up at the station just a mile from our home, we were determined to love her as if she were our own daughter. We offered to let her stay in our spare bedroom to save her the cost of meals and lodging, and this gave us the opportunity to give her some much needed love and attention. She perked up and immersed herself in the workshop, fully participating in the meditations and healing exercises.

By the end of the workshop, three different people who possessed gifts of spiritual sensitivity independently received the message that Katia desperately needed a respite of two weeks' time to heal and recharge her batteries. I began to wrestle with the question of how and where this could take place, not to mention the question of whether or not she would be able to get the time off of work and support from her husband. After discussing it with another medium who was in attendance at my workshop, we realized that the absolute best situation would be for her to continue staying as a guest in my home. That would require approval from Connie; it would be asking a lot of her to be hostess to a severely depressed young woman for two weeks. I talked it over with her and was deeply moved by Connie's compassionate heart when she agreed to take up the challenge.

Then I needed to present the idea to Katia. During a break in the workshop, I went for a little walk with her and we wound up talking about it at the end of our driveway. Synchronistically, at the exact moment I told Katia that the spirit world had informed us that what she needed was to be taken care of in the way parents would lovingly take care of a child, Connie unexpectedly came out of the house and called to her, "Katia, why don't you come in and have some tea? I'll be your mother." That really got Katia's attention. She felt it was a sign and made the decision to see if she could arrange to stay. I was amazed when after a few phone calls she said that she had the "green light" to go ahead and stay.

Two significant things happened during the two weeks Katia was with us that helped her immensely. They both came about through mediumship. We were given information from the other side that revealed the pathway to her healing. First, we came to understand that part of the reason for Katia's depression had to do with her paternal grandfather. From the spirit side, her grandfather was attached to her with the motivation and intention of protecting her, but in attempting to do so he created some unintended consequences. We received that he had been a soldier in the Soviet Army during World War II. During his service, he had been involved in some military actions that included atrocities against civilians in which he participated. Even though these things had taken place decades earlier, he was still wracked by guilt and remorse for his actions. In fact, even in the spirit world, he was suffering from depression. Because he was so close to his grand-daughter on the earth plane, the energy of his depressed mind was pulling her down as well. The situation was similar to the way my Sicilian grandfather affected my moods by causing me to get angry at my children.

Connie and I held a prayer circle with Katia where we invited the white light of the Holy Spirit to descend and open a beautiful portal that enabled Katia's grandfather to detach himself from her and ascend into the Light.

The second incident took place just before she was to return to New York. Katia confessed to me that another thing that troubled her was dealing with anger. She said that there were times when she would be talking with her husband, the discussion would result in some disagreement, and then escalate into an argument in which she would feel an overwhelming and uncontrollable anger that shocked her.

"Katia," I asked. "When this happens to you, do you feel like yourself, or does it feel like somebody else."

"No," she replied. "I don't feel like myself when this happens. That's why it scares me."

Through mediumship, we ascertained that there was another spirit hanging around Katia. This spirit was a little boy. He had died during World War II, and for some reason had not ascended into the spirit world. The anger was coming from him. He was angry that he had been separated from his mother.

Connie and I held another prayer ceremony with Katia. Again, we invited the white light of the Holy Spirit to descend. This time I saw the boy's deceased mother descend through the light and greet him. He went to his mother and ascended into the light. I don't understand completely why these phenomena take place. For example, I don't know why this particular boy was attached to Katia, but I do have a suspicion. I think that this boy and his mother were somehow connected to the atrocities committed by Katia's grandfather during World War II.

When the two weeks were over, we took a rejuvenated and hopeful Katia to the Amtrak station. There were tears and hugs all around, and we sent her off with hopes that her life would improve. When I spoke to her a few days later, she said that her suicidal ideation had completely stopped, and I am so relieved to report that, years later, Katia is still with us. In the time that has passed she has found better employment, a better living situation, and a wonderful artistic outlet by creating children's books in her spare time. I am so grateful for this outcome; I've always been a sucker for stories that have happy endings.

22 - Miracle Healings

By this time, I had joined a spiritualist church called the First United Metaphysical Chapel in Bahama, North Carolina. Within a few weeks, I was asked to serve as an assistant pastor there. I was also asked to serve as a spiritual healer because I had recently completed my training to become a certified Reiki master. American Spiritualists perform hands-on healing, and there is some over-lapping similarity with Reiki, a hands-on healing modality which originated in Japan.

Spiritual healings are something that I still don't fully under-stand, but because they are another activity associated with mediumship, I feel like I should share some of the things I have learned so far.

In my youth as a Roman Catholic schoolboy, I was fascinated by the many healings that Jesus performed. He didn't just heal people over time, but sometimes immediately with just the touch of a hand. Sometimes he could heal someone who wasn't even in his physical presence, healing over long distances. I had some limited experience with that during my Reiki training; we were taught techniques that facilitated healing at a distance. So, the things Jesus did don't surprise me, and although this may surprise the reader, I believe that all human beings have the potential to develop to the point where they can perform them as well.

I attended Reiki gatherings regularly for at least a couple of years and receiving a Reiki treatment was always a very pleasant experience. A group of us who had various levels of training gathered every week and held sessions where we'd take turns laying down on a massage table while several practitioners would lay hands on us at the same time. The healers would spread their hands out so almost the entire body of the person on the table would be covered with hands. The person receiving this kind of treatment never wanted it to end! At a minimum, they would experience wonderful feelings such as a very warm soothing energy flowing from the Reiki practitioners' hands. Calming, relaxing, peacefulness, serenity, safety, and a feeling of "I'm at home here" are some of the words I would use to describe the Reiki experience.

Sometimes, the recipient receives a feeling of deep love and embrace. I have a friend who told me that the first time he had several Reiki practitioners lay hands on him, he was so over-whelmed that he burst into uncontrollable weeping. They weren't painful tears at all. They were more like tears of release and reunion, accompanied by a feeling of total love and acceptance. The loving energy seems to be coming from a source above and beyond the practitioners themselves.

My own Reiki experience piqued my curiosity to understand more about how the body could be healed through various spiritual healing modalities. Reiki was a gentle form of spiritual healing that usually took more than one treatment to produce significant results. I knew beyond a shadow of a doubt that there was something energetic going on, because through Reiki I acquired the ability to do something that the average person might consider miraculous. If I were watching TV with my family and the remote control stopped working because it needed a new battery, I could simply take the batteries into my hands and focus my energy on them for a couple of minutes, and they would start working again for a while. Usually, the recharging only lasted for a few days, and we'd wind up putting a new battery in anyway. I did this a few times for the batteries in clocks, and they would recharge for weeks. When a clock would stop working, I'd ask someone to take it down, give me the battery, and I'd recharge it. On one occasion I did this at the Triangle Family Church in Durham, and every time I returned the clock was still working for at least many weeks afterwards.

Recharging an AA battery is no earth-shattering feat, but it's not normal. It was convincing evidence to me that there was some unseen healing force available to humanity if we just learned how to harness and channel it.

There were a handful of occasions where people told me they felt immediately better when I performed hands-on healing for them, such as a headache disappearing or muscle pain going away. On one occasion I was asked to help a couple of other healing ministers perform healing to a woman who was bedridden at Duke Medical Center. She had been hospitalized for cancer treatment and the medical workers had accidentally given her the wrong medicine, causing a toxic reaction in her body. She was a woman of very strong faith and had implored the church to send healers to her. As I raised my hands above her, I could feel an unusually strong energy pouring through me out to the woman. My body became so hot that even though the room was air conditioned my whole body was drenched with sweat by the time I had finished. The woman recovered and was discharged from the hospital the next day.

Even though I had some success with healing, I wanted more. I aspired to be like Jesus, as he promised.[21] I wanted to develop to

---

[21] John 14:12 (NRSV)

the point where I could just touch someone and heal them instantaneously.

I witnessed such a spontaneous healing take place when I attended a gathering of Pentecostal Christians in Wilkesboro, North Carolina, at a three-day long seminar called the "Seer Anointing" organized by a ministerial group including the married team of Kevin and Kathy Basconi. I was attracted to the conference without knowing it had anything to do with healing, but because of my interest in basic mediumship. The Christian term for mediumship is "the gift of prophecy." A "seer" is one who possesses the gift of prophecy, so that's why the topic of the conference immediately grabbed my attention.

During the course of this seminar, healing services were held. Christian ministers who had decades of experience in this field officiated. After one such service, I overheard a woman saying that her knee had been instantaneously healed. I view myself as a person with a scientific mindset, so I was eager to investigate this woman's experience in more detail. I waited until the next day and asked her if she would be willing to speak to me about her experience; I was curious to see if the healing had any permanence to it. I thought it might have been just a temporary feeling in the heat of the moment.

The woman kindly agreed, and we found a quiet spot where we could talk away from the large crowd of participants. She was a well-dressed woman who looked to be in her forties and was well-articulated in her speech.

"Yesterday, I heard you tell your companions that you had received a spontaneous healing when the minister prayed for you. How did you know that you had been healed?" I asked.

"Well," she thought for a moment, "because the pain went away."

"Is the pain still gone?"

"Yes, my knee still feels fine."

"Can you tell me about what's been going on with your knee?"

"Well, it had been giving me problems for a long time. The pain had gotten to the point where I realized I needed to have surgery. I have actually scheduled the surgery, but then I found out about this seminar. So, I decided to come here and give this a try first."

The woman is a Registered Nurse (RN), so a lot of her friends and colleagues are also in the medical profession. When she mentioned she had scheduled the surgery, I could tell that the topic made her feel uncomfortable, and I wondered why. What she said next really convinced me that her story was genuine.

"I don't know what I'm going to do when I go back to work," she said. "I don't know how I'm going to explain to people why I'm canceling my knee surgery."

23 - Crescentia's Miraculous Healing

I've facilitated spontaneous healings on a few occasions, and in 2019 I had the opportunity to perform a healing and also interview the recipient a couple of days afterwards.

I had traveled to New York City to take an intensive class on "The Life and Teachings of Jesus" with the Rev. Dr. Jacob David as part of the program for completing my master's degree in religious education at the Unification Theological Seminary in Manhattan. I was excited not only because of the topic, but also because it was a fun adventure to drive up from my home in North Carolina and spend a week in New York during the springtime.

On the first morning of the class, I saw a young woman student named Crescentia DeGoede walk into our classroom in noticeable pain, and limping. She had gone camping with her family, and on the hike down she severely twisted her ankle.

After making a mental note to talk to her about performing hands-on healing when a chance presented itself, I caught up to her during a break in the class. She agreed to allow me to perform a healing prayer with her. The healing was immediately and completely successful. Two days later, I asked her if she would allow me to videotape an interview with her to record her experience. Crescentia graciously agreed. Here is an excerpt from the transcript (edited for clarity):

Ron: I noticed right away that you were limping when you came in (last Monday).

Crescentia: Yeah, so even (when) I made the walk to class I was walking really, really slowly because I could feel the tenderness in the ankle. When I got to class, I didn't want to mess it up any further. So, when I first sat down, I put my leg up.

Ron: I remember you asked the professor "Is it okay if I put my leg up?"

Crescentia: Yeah, I felt funny about it, but I realized that I have to take care of it.

Ron: It looks great now!

Crescentia: Yeah, you can even see a remnant of where the bruise was.

Ron: Alright, so then what happened?

Crescentia: So, you said, "Well, let's do a healing."

Ron: "Let's do a prayer."

Crescentia: Yeah, "Let's do a healing prayer, later." I thought you were kidding. Usually somebody says that to you and it's kind of a joke. But you were serious!

Ron: Yeah, I was dead serious.

Crescentia: (She laughs) You were serious, and then I believe it was (during) the first break that we had.

Ron: I think so.

Crescentia: You came over and you offered to do the prayer and you explained about the healing ability, that if the person who is receiving the healing can believe that God can instantly (snaps her fingers) heal someone then that person can be healed.

Ron: Yeah, it can happen.

Crescentia: It can happen. So, then you began. I believe you kind of just hovered your hand over my knee, my leg, and started to pray for the healing of my ankle, and as you were praying, actually, I was visualizing the ankle, and I was visualizing your healing energy going to the ankle and allowing myself to be open to God healing that. Picturing my ankle being healed, whole, and healthy, and just also trying to receive this love, this positive energy that was coming through you for the healing of my ankle. Then the prayer ended, and I opened my eyes and I think you asked me, "How does it feel?"

Ron: Yeah, what I did is I touched you on your leg and I said, "Be healed!"

Crescentia: Right!

Ron: And that was the end of it. And then you opened your eyes.

Crescentia: Yeah, I opened my eyes and immediately I kind of moved it around to try to see, well, how does it feel now, and it was strange to see that it instantly had felt better. Since then, that was Monday, now we're at Wednesday, and for the past two days I've walked to and from class fifteen minutes each way and I don't feel any pain.

Ron: Are you limping anymore?

Crescentia: There's like a little bit of tenderness, a slight tenderness, but I'm not limping . . . .

Crescentia went on to say that prior to the healing she had been planning to talk to her boss about canceling a trip to Las Vegas to work at a program there. Because of the pain in her ankle, she knew she wouldn't be able to walk or stand as required for the event, but the healing assured her that she would be able to make the trip after all.

Crescentia: And then you offered this healing and since then it's been better and now there's no question; I can do the program.

Ron: Wow! That's cool.

Crescentia: ...Yeah, in Las Vegas. So, it's pretty, I mean the word that comes to mind is it's unbelievable. (She laughs)

Ron: Alright, so how about emotionally. What did you feel in the moment? When you said that during the prayer, while I was praying, you were also really focused, and you were open to receive? What did you feel emotionally in your heart at any time during that process, especially when you realized that it was better? What did you feel at that moment?

Crescentia: Gratitude. Just gratefulness. Warmth.

Ron: Did you choke up at all?

Crescentia: Yeah.

Ron: Did you really?

Crescentia: Yeah

Ron: That's a good sign.

Crescentia: I definitely felt warmth and kind of like a peacefulness.

Ron: Peacefulness.

Crescentia: Yeah, that I'm in good hands and that this is—it's interesting because what I could feel was that God was present and I just needed to get into the presence of God.

Ron: Yes.

Crescentia: If I could get into that—feel that presence of God—and so I was just sort of, through the prayer, surrendering myself to that presence of God, and letting God be there in my ankle, essentially.

Ron: Well, in my view, you just hit the nail on the head because that's what I've always felt is that God is always present. It's just a matter of whether we can get ourselves into that same vibration into the presence of God and then the "magic" happens.

Crescentia: Yeah.

Ron: Well, thank you so much . . . I really, really appreciate you sharing your testimony like this.

Crescentia: Thank you, Ron. I appreciate you sharing your healing ability.

Ron: Well, God shared his healing ability through me. It wasn't me. God bless you. Thanks.

Crescentia reported that she felt "peacefulness," "warmth," and that she was "in good hands." (I felt that she meant God's hands.) I'm actually more excited about these feelings than I am about the healing of her ankle. Physical injuries come, then heal, and the memory of the pain of them fades in time, but she will never forget the emotional feelings she experienced during this healing.

During the prophetic exercises I teach at my workshops and training seminars, whether during hands-on healing or guided meditation, almost universally participants report a feeling of "peace" and "calm." In my view, this is a sign that they have entered into the vibration of God. If they go deeper into the experience, they will get to the point where Crescentia felt she was "in good hands." This means they have penetrated to the point where they are experiencing not just the peace and calm of God, but also a feeling that they are "home" and "safe" in the presence of God, and with this they will feel the love of God. At that point, usually they begin to weep. They realize that God is a God of love, but not just as a concept. They experience that God loves them personally, and that they are worthy to receive this love. That can be a life-transformative experience, and in my view, that realization is far more valuable than the physical healing itself.

24 - Give a Healing, Get a Healing

Many of us who practice various forms of healing modalities have a maxim or saying that we repeat to each other on occasion, "Give a healing, get a healing." What we mean is that during the course of performing spiritual healing on someone we sometimes experience a healing ourselves.

One analogy I use to describe this phenomenon is the analogy of the garden hose. While the purpose of a garden hose is to channel water from a source to the plants growing in the garden, during that transmission the inside of the garden hose also gets wet as the water passes through it. In the same way, during hands-on healing the healer is a conduit for the healing power of the Holy Spirit to pass through them. Just as the garden hose gets wet with water, the hands-on healer gets "wet" with the Holy Spirit.

For example, most practitioners will feel a warmth or tingling in their hands while performing hands-on healing. Many report that the warming or tingling begins even before they lay their hands on someone; it certainly does in my case. Beyond the physical feeling of warmth or tingling, there are spiritual and emotional feelings that sometimes pass through us as well. Often times those who receive a hands-on healing will experience a profound sense of Divine love in addition to the healing energy. This love can be so powerful that the recipient is moved deeply and begins to weep. If the healer also senses this Divine love in the course of giving a healing, they might begin to weep as well.

This is what happened to me one Sunday morning when I was performing healings at the First United Metaphysical Chapel. At the start of each service, we placed a handful of chairs in the front of the sanctuary and invited any member of the congregation who wanted to come forward and receive a hands-on healing.

In those days, I had almost no experience meeting or interacting with people who were not heterosexual in their orientation. To make matters worse, my religious upbringing left me with a lingering belief system that branded practicing homo-sexuals as horrible sinners, and I was indoctrinated to believe that they were all destined for eternal damnation in Hell. Needless to say, I was uncomfortable with the whole subject of homosexuality and homosexuals.

As an assistant pastor, I felt that I had a responsibility to do my best to love all of the members unconditionally. This conviction was challenged when I discovered that one of my congregants was an openly lesbian woman. My religious education told me that this woman was engaging in an inherently sinful lifestyle, but my heart was having a hard time accepting that. This woman was a very loving person. She had been previously married to a man with whom she was still on good terms, and they had given birth to a beautiful teenaged daughter who sometimes accompanied her to church. On a couple of occasions, her ex-husband attended and the three of them sat together in church. I was moved by this woman's sincerity and her commitment to do the best she could to exemplify love in her relationship with her ex-husband and her daughter.

On one Sunday morning, the minister in charge of the healing service announced to the congregation that it was time for anyone to come forward who wanted a healing. So, while I was standing behind one of the chairs, ready for someone to come up, the lesbian woman stood up from her pew. I could tell by the way she was walking that she was making a beeline directly to my chair. I was already in healing mode before she stood up—my hands had warmed up—and my heart was welling up with compassion towards the congregation. As she began walking towards me, I felt the spirit of God was within me, and as I looked at her it was as if I was looking at her with the eyes of God. In that moment I saw her simply as a precious child of God, walking towards my chair with an open heart of sincerity and humility hoping to receive a personal healing. I began to choke up. My heart swelled with overwhelming love for her. She took her seat in my chair, and I lay my hands on her shoulders. The moment I touched her, the voice of God spoke in my heart saying, "This is my beloved daughter, in whom I am well pleased." I immediately recognized that these were the same sentiments God expressed to Jesus when he was baptized at the Jordan River. I was blown away by the beauty and the power of Divine love. I knew beyond a shadow of a doubt that this woman's sexual orientation—and anyone's orientation for that matter—had no bearing at all on the profound love that God has for each person.

In that moment my heart was also healed. My intuitive suspicion that my religious upbringing was incorrect was affirmed, and I felt a sense of liberation. I felt that from now on I was free to love anyone without judgment. This experience literally changed my life and set me free.

25 - Mediums Are Not Always Right

A few years ago, Connie and I hosted a monthly *spirit circle* in our home. A few people would come by, and after sharing some food and chatting for a while, we practiced giving messages from the spirit world to each other. We had a regular group of half a dozen or so, but from time to time the group would expand to more than a dozen people.

On one occasion, one of the participants was a woman who was not a part of the regular group. Her name was Rita, and as is often the case with those seeking communication from the spirit world, she had recently lost a family member. In her case, it was her teenaged daughter. Rita came in and took a seat on the sofa in our living room. After the group shared in some refreshments, I agreed to do what is called a *gallery reading*. Those who are familiar with the work of the famous American medium John Edward will recognize the format of a gallery reading.

In most cases, readings are done in a one-on-one format. There is one medium, and there is one sitter, but in a gallery reading there may be only one medium, but there is a group of people sitting with the medium hoping for a message. These types of readings are more difficult to do, because the medium oftentimes does not know exactly which participant is the intended target of any spirit messages they receive. At times it can get a little confusing.

For example, the medium might receive through *clairaudience* a particular name like "James." So, the medium will say to the group "I'm receiving the name James, does anyone here have someone in the spirit world named James?" Since James is such a common name, it would not be unusual for several people to raise their hands, so the medium has to make further effort to discern which James is communicating. How would the medium do that? At that point, what often happens is the spirit will send a second piece of information to help with identification. For example, the medium might then receive an image in their mind through *clairvoyance* of a head with wavy red hair on top.

"Can anyone identify with a James that had wavy red hair?" the medium would ask. At that point, if only one person remains with their hand raised, the medium knows this person is the intended recipient of this particular message.

It can be a difficult business. Sometimes the information given seems to be incorrect; I don't clearly understand why that happens, but it does. At other times the information is correctly given from the spirit, but it is not communicated correctly by the medium. Thirdly, sometimes the information is communicated correctly, but the intended recipient doesn't recognize it for whatever reason.

The message I gave to Rita is a perfect example of the second case: the information I received was correctly given from the spirit, but I did not communicate it correctly.

Rita had been quietly sitting in the same spot on the sofa throughout the evening and remained there as I began the gallery reading. I stood up, closed my eyes, and waited to see if I would receive anything. Immediately I saw an image in my mind's eye that appeared to be a toy pickup truck, with a large full bunch of celery standing upright in the back of the truck. I thought to myself, "What in the world is this? This makes absolutely no sense."

Fortunately, one of my mentors, a very accomplished medium named Philip Burley, taught me that if I was to be a successful medium, I had to be willing to risk making a fool of myself. I was also taught that it wasn't my responsibility to make sense of the information, but it was my responsibility to honestly and clearly relay the messages I received to the best of my ability. In obedience to his instructions, I opened my mouth and simply revealed the image I had in my mind:

"I'm seeing a toy pickup truck with a bunch of celery standing up in the back of the truck. The stems of the celery are pointing up, and I can see the leaves bushing out at the top. Does this make sense to anybody?"

To my stunned amazement, Rita calmly said, "Oh yes. It makes sense to me."

I focused in on Rita, dying to hear her explanation of this bizarre image.

"You see," she explained. "I work in a florist shop. I make flower arrangements. Sometimes I will take a toy pickup truck, and I will arrange a bunch of flowers in the back of the truck bed."

"Wow," I thought. "That actually makes sense." I can see that if a little boy were in the hospital, this would be the perfect kind of flower arrangement to send to him. He could enjoy the flowers, and then take the toy truck home with him when he left the hospital. Brilliant!

At this point in a reading, an interesting phenomenon often takes place within me. Now that I felt certain I had connected to the person the spirit was trying to communicate with, my connection to the spirit became stronger. It's hard to explain, but it's as if an electrical connection had been plugged in. So, after Rita explained the meaning of the toy pickup truck, I immediately received a second image.

"Rita," I said. "I'm seeing a trellis. You know that wooden structure you often see in gardens. And there are roses growing on this trellis. Also, I can see that this rose trellis is growing next to the door of a house. Does that make sense to you?"

"Oh, yes. My mother lived in Italy, and she had a trellis like this growing by her front door."

Now the reading was increasing in energy. I was certain that the spirit that was communicating was Rita's deceased mother. I could sense her presence. At this point, the reading moved beyond clairvoyance and clairaudience, to *clairsentience*. Clairsentience means "clear feeling." The connection was strong now, and, somehow, I just knew what Rita's mother wanted to say to her.

"Rita, your mom is here. She just wants you to know how happy she is that you are working in the flower shop. She says it's really wonderful that you have a job in which you have the opportunity to express your creativity through your work. She says that it's really good for you."

Along with the message, I could empathetically feel Rita's mother's emotions. I could feel how much love she had for her daughter. It was a deeply moving experience not just for Rita, but also for me.

Now that I've shared this story, let's take a closer look at the phenomenon I mentioned above about how information can be correctly given from the spirit, but not communicated correctly by the medium.

In the case of Rita's mother, I'm fairly certain that she intended to impress my brain with an image of a flower arrangement in the back of a toy pickup truck. That image originates in the spirit world, and with the help of other spirits who are adept at spirit communication, Rita's mother sent that image to my brain the way a television station might broadcast the image of a flower arrangement to your TV set.

Just as a TV image can be blurred or otherwise interfered with by factors like the weather, electrical or other technical problems, the image transmitted to my brain can be interfered with as well, making it difficult to see precisely all the details of the image. In my case, even though I'm sure Rita's mother transmitted an image including a flower arrangement, my brain interpreted it as a bunch of celery. If you Google an image of a bunch of celery, you will see that the shape is almost the same as that of a flower arrangement. In both cases, the bottom will consist of stems rising vertically into a canopy of broader foliage. While the shape is similar, the color is different. While both the celery and the flower arrangement will have green stems from the bottom rising up, the celery leaves will be green at the top while the flower arrangement will be of a different color or colors. For some reason, my brain did not perceive the color on the top, and so it translated the image as a bunch of celery instead of as a flower arrangement.

I'm trying to impress on the reader just how easy it can be for a medium to give incorrect or slightly altered information. It also demonstrates how important it is for the medium and the sitter to work together as partners. The sitter is not just a passive observer but can greatly facilitate the process of mediumship. First, there are things a sitter can do in the days or weeks before a scheduled reading to prepare for a successful reading; I'll reveal those in the next chapter. Secondly, by understanding the process of mediumship, the sitter can help as well.

For example, if Rita had a completely skeptical mind about mediumship, she might have thought the idea of celery in a pickup truck was just absurd. Fortunately, because she had a mind that was more open to the possibility of spirit communication, she was able to see the connection between what I was receiving and her occupation as a florist. If she hadn't done that, I would have simply moved on to another message for a different sitter, and the opportunity for her mother to make her presence known and share the beautiful uplifting message for her daughter would have been completely lost.

Message opportunities are also often lost when the information given is correct, but the sitter doesn't recognize it. For example: during my readings, spirits of parents have sometimes shared information that took place during the sitter's childhood, but because the sitter was so young at the time, he or she has lost any memory of the event. Even though the event was deeply mean-ingful to the parent, the assumption that it remains just as meaningful to the child is mistaken. Sometimes during the reading the child cannot make sense of the information coming from their parent, but days later they have a realization of what the parent was referring to.

It's important to remember that spirits are just ordinary human beings who no longer have physical bodies. Many of their unique personality traits, ways of communicating, beliefs, biases, and eccentricities remain intact even after crossing over into the next life. These can have an effect on how well a spirit communicates during a reading. I have noticed that I often have an easier time relaying messages from people in the spirit world who are like me. My father was an Italian immigrant, and I have inherited his loud voice, animated manner of speaking, and gregarious nature. I love being around people, and I don't have a problem baring my soul or speaking in front of a large crowd. On the other hand, if a person was shy, introverted, or otherwise very guarded in their communi-cation in life, they can be a more difficult person for me to get communication from when they cross over to the other side.

26 - How to Prepare for a Reading with a Medium

A few years ago, I did a reading for a young woman whose teenaged ex-boyfriend had recently committed suicide. Even though they were no longer a couple, they remained friends, and the young lady told me the reason she wanted to have the reading was just "to see if he was okay," but she didn't tell me there was more to it than that. As we were getting towards the end of the reading, I had not received anything related to her deceased boyfriend. I didn't see an image of him, receive any words or symbols, or any other sign of his presence. As time was running out, I said to him telepathically something I had never said before or since to a spirit, "Don't be a jerk! This is your ex-girlfriend, for crying out loud. Don't you have anything you want to say to her?" He eventually responded with one sentence, clear as a bell, "Everybody is angry with me." That's the only thing I could get him to say. I conveyed the message to his ex-girlfriend, and then I asked her a question.

"Young lady," I said, "have you forgiven (ex-boyfriend's name) yet?"

"Well," she replied, hesitatingly. "Sometimes I'm still angry with him."

Imagine just a normal teenaged boy living in your neighborhood that goes to the local high school. He's just done something really stupid that has caused his ex-girlfriend to be deeply hurt. He had no intention of hurting her, but now he finds out that she's angry and is driving over to his house because she wants to talk to him. Would we be surprised if the boy jumped into his car and drove away to avoid the confrontation? Of course not. Then why should we be surprised when the spirit of a teenage boy who has recently committed suicide is reluctant to talk to his ex-girlfriend who is angry with him? Remember, spirits are just ordinary human beings who no longer have physical bodies. They think, feel and act in very similar ways as they would when they were still on the earth.

The point of this story is that there are things that we can do in preparation if we want to be successful in establishing meaningful communication with the spirit of a deceased loved one. One of the most powerful ways is to forgive. If we have any lingering feelings of regret or resentment towards the deceased person, it can impede our attempt to establish communication.

Send loving thoughts to the person. You can speak directly to them, and they can receive your words even though you may not sense their presence. If you have a photo of them, you can talk to the photo. I will even kiss Josh's photo occasionally. He has told us that these loving thoughts, gestures, and prayers have a powerful beneficial effect on him and others in the spirit world. Pray for their highest good. Pray that they might be at peace and be liberated from any feelings of regret or remorse. Tell them you love them. Tell them you hold no grudges against them for the past, and ask them to forgive you for anything you might have done to hurt them.

Another thing we can do to facilitate spirit communication is to formulate whatever questions we may have and write them down long before the reading. One time I asked a famous person who had recently passed into the spirit world if he would allow me to interview him for a book at a later date through the service of another gifted medium I was working with. He agreed, but he asked me to formulate the questions I would ask him during the interview at least two weeks before the reading. I found that interesting. I believe it gives the spirits time to figure out the best way to answer the questions so that the responses may be communicated as accurately as possible.

Afterwards, I began asking my sitters to do the same thing. A woman from Maryland contacted me because her sister had recently crossed over. She had a few questions she wanted to ask her sister, so I asked her to write them down immediately, keep them by her bedside, and reread them at least once a day until the day of the reading. When the time came for the reading, I began by sharing the impressions I was already receiving from her sister. When I finished, I told the woman she could now ask her questions. She replied, "You just answered every question I had written down here on my legal pad."

One thing you don't want to do is tell the medium details relating to the person you are hoping to get in contact with. I don't like it when people do this; it actually makes my job more difficult. Sometimes I'm given information like this: "My sister Mary just passed away. She died from a heart attack three months ago. Her birthday is January 1, 1975. I'm really upset because we were so close, we were like twins. She was in poor health for a long time, and I feel so guilty for not taking better care of her towards the end of her life. Do you think you can help me get in touch with her?"

The reason I don't like this is because these are details that spirits often communicate to me during a reading in order to identify themselves. If I give you some of these bits of information during the reading without knowing anything in advance, it's a very powerful demonstration of evidentiary mediumship. A person's name, age, when they died, how they died, their relationship to you before they died—these are all things that a spirit will often try to communicate to try to identify themselves during a reading. But if you tell me all this before I do the reading, I'm not sure if I'm saying these things because I'm remembering what you told me, or if I'm actually getting communication from the spirit you're trying to get in touch with.

It is okay to say something like this, "There is someone in the spirit world I would like to get in touch with, and I'm wondering if you can help me with that." Notice here that there is no mention of the person's name, timing, their relationship to you, or even their gender. So, you're not giving anything away by making this kind of request.

Here is a copy of an email I send out to people who schedule a reading with me, explaining more about what to expect:

Dear Friend,

I wanted to send you this letter to explain what I do so you have a clear understanding of what to expect from a reading with me.

I am a clairvoyant, clairaudient, and clairsentient medium. What that means is that I "see" symbols, images, and words, "hear" words and sometimes complete sentences, and "feel" emotions and sentiments that spirits want to convey to you, the sitter.

I am not like a telephone carrying on direct conversations with spirits and then repeating this information back to the sitter. Oftentimes, I simply receive symbols, images, words, and or feelings which have no meaning to me as the medium, but which, unknown to me, are very meaningful to the sitter. My responsibility is simply to convey what I receive as best I can.

I have little control over who will communicate in a particular reading. That is decided by God and those in the Spirit World. If I was having a reading with a medium myself, though I might like to receive a message from my mother, if it is better for me to receive a message from my paternal grandfather, then that's who is going to come through. I cannot guarantee who will come through. However, I can ask for specific people to come through and oftentimes they do.

My favorite part of this work is conveying the messages I receive about you from God, because these are the messages that are the best ones for you to know for your own spiritual path. In the readings, you receive what is for your highest good, and what comes through may be a pleasant surprise to you.

If you haven't done so already, you are welcome to read some of the testimonies from others who have had readings with me to give you more ideas of what to expect. If for any reason you are unhappy with the reading, I will refund your fee. I wanted to clearly explain this so you don't have a misconception about what I do. One thing I can guarantee is that your reading will be a very profound experience that will benefit your life.

It is a holy, sacred experience, as those who come through are only interested in your highest well-being and good.

Infinite Blessings to you and your family!

Most Sincerely,

Ron

27 - Rescue Me

Another type of work that mediums do is called *rescue mediumship*. It is the process of assisting spirits who are trapped on the earth plane to finally ascend into the spirit world. Spirits sometimes remain on the earth after their physical body dies for various reasons. There are mediums who specialize in helping such spirits cross over into the spirit world. There was even a Canadian-produced television show about it called *Rescue Mediums* that ran from 2006 to 2011.

As bizarre as this may sound, some spirits remain on the earth because they don't realize that they are dead. Sometimes it's because they are committed to the ideology of materialism. Because this belief system is so strongly ingrained within their conscious-ness, they do not recognize their own deaths. There is no room in their thought process to entertain the idea of a life after physical death or the existence of a spiritual realm. Therefore, when they find themselves still possessing their own personal consciousness, as well as a spiritual body, they convince themselves that they must still be physically alive. They stay on the earth, usually in the residence they were occupying at the time of their physical death and continue living there as if nothing has happened. Sometimes, when their home gets put on the market and a new resident moves in, they do everything they can to try to drive the new resident out. This is one of the scenarios behind the phenomenon referred to as a *haunted house*. I would not refer to these tenacious residents as evil spirits; from their point of view, the new owners are trespassing in their home. That is a reasonable conclusion for someone who doesn't know that their physical life has come to an end. If someone moved into your home uninvited, you probably wouldn't be happy about it either.

My favorite story about one of these earthbound spirits comes from Peru. It's a story that began over 350 years ago during the time after Peru's indigenous peoples, the Incas, began to be violently subjugated by Spanish conquistadores, a process that continued for over forty years. The natives were no match for the Spanish soldiers with their armor, guns, and horses.

Along with the soldiers came Roman Catholic priests and monks. They arrived ostensibly to save the souls of the Inca people by converting them to Christianity, but sometimes they got caught between the violence of the soldiers and the purpose of their calling.

The capital of the Incan Empire was the Peruvian city of Cusco, high up in the Andes mountains. The Spaniards made it their capital after the conquest, and Cusco is the scene of this ghost story. The haunting takes place in a large home that was built more than 350 years ago. In its heyday, it had been the home of a Spanish nobleman. One of the people who stayed for a time in this elaborate residence was a Catholic monk, and it was he who made the decision to stay in his room long after the death of his physical body.

Fast forward to the twenty-first century. A psychotherapist named Caron B. Goode visited Cusco, and rented a room in the converted colonial building that just happened to be the same room this monk died in so many years before.

The monk made his presence known to Ms. Goode by interfering with the hot water in her room, preventing her from being able to take a much-needed shower. After getting her attention, the monk explained to her that he had died in this room hundreds of years ago, knew he was dead, but refrained from ascending into the spiritual world because he was afraid that he would be sent to Hell for his sins. He had become involved in the killing of others, at least some of whom were indigenous peoples, and then began to enjoy the act of killing. For whatever reason, he had arrived at the moment where he was ready to ascend and face whatever fate was in store for him, and asked Ms. Goode to help him.

She called upon angels for assistance, and a warmness and light filled up the room. The monk saw the light, walked into it, and disappeared. Afterwards, everything in the room returned to normal, and Ms. Goode was able to partake of a much-deserved hot shower.[22]

I have performed rescue mediumship when called upon. One case took place in March of 2019. A friend of mine named Lois wrote to me asking for help involving some disturbing activity that was taking place in a home in a middle-class subdivision a few miles east of where I live. An acquaintance of Lois had recently bought a home with her husband. They had a young son, and after the family moved in the child began having trouble sleeping. He said there was a teenaged boy in his room who began talking to him. It wasn't just a one-time encounter. Understandably, this was disturbing to the little boy.

His mother began to suspect that a spirit was bothering her son. She did a little research and discovered that the family that

---

[22] Caron B. Goode. *Kids Who See Ghosts: How to Guide Them Through Fear.* San Francisco: Weiser Books. 2010. pp.24-26.

owned the home before they moved in had suffered the loss of their teenaged son to suicide. Their little boy was sleeping in the teenager's former bedroom. Putting two and two together, she surmised that the suicidal teenager was probably the one who was troubling her son.

Connie and I arranged to visit the home to see if we could be of assistance. We were greeted warmly by the mother who showed us around the house and explained all the goings on in great detail. I spent about half an hour talking to and playing with the little boy in his room. He was very happy to show me around and tell me all about his different toys. I didn't question him or mention anything about the teenaged spirit, I just wanted to see how he was doing.

When I felt the time was right, I suggested that we conduct a prayer circle right there in the middle of the bedroom. The little boy's aunt took him outside to play so we could proceed undisturbed. Connie and I invited the mother to join hands with us and we said a prayer for the liberation of the spirit of the teenage boy. We invited the white light of the Holy Spirit to descend into the room. This creates a kind of doorway or portal into the spiritual world, through which spirits will descend such as grandparents or other entities, such as angels, who have a great love for the teen suicide. Then, we spoke to the teenager and invited him to walk into the light. That's all there is to it; it's not that complicated.

While touring the house we noticed that the mother had displayed some of her artwork in a couple of places. They had been created when she was a troubled teenager herself. Although the technique was excellent, the content was dark and moody. One that was hanging in the bathroom was particularly disturbing. The art was meaningful to her because, first of all, the technique was good, but we were concerned about the negative energy it might be bringing into the home, because it demonstrated a time when she was going through deep emotional struggles.

We told her she didn't need to get rid of the art. We recommended she take it down and put it in a portfolio for safekeeping. We encouraged her to create a new painting of a subject that was uplifting and inspiring. She thought this was a great idea, and later sent us a copy of a beautiful Angel that she had used to replace the dark picture in the bathroom.

A few days after we performed the prayer circle exercise, I texted the mother to see how things were going. She told me that life in their home had immediately returned to normal. Her son was sleeping well, and there were no further episodes of the teenage boy visiting him in his room.

I'm still surprised at how easy it can often be to help a spirit cross over to the other side. I wish more people were aware of this simple technique and willing to give it a try. It would lead to peace for many troubled spirits, and to more peace in the world.

28 - How Do You Find a Good Medium?

People often ask me if there are any mediums I recommend. Most people don't know where to begin to find a good medium. In my experience, most mediums are found through word of mouth. If you're looking for a medium, talk to people you respect. Ask them if they've ever used a medium, and if they can give you a recommendation. You will be surprised to find out how many people have used mediums at some point in their life, but it's not something they're going to talk about unless asked. In some circles there is still a stigma attached to going to a medium.

There are people who are called certified mediums. Those are mediums who have been tested. The National Spiritualist Association of Churches (NSAC) has a certification process. The way they test mediums is by having them do a reading for every single board member of the association. The medium will have to give evidentiary information to the members before they can be officially certified. The medium has to tell each board member something related to them that the medium could not possibly have known and only the board member recognizes as true. That provides evidence that the medium is truly communicating with the spirit world and not just imagining things. Only then will mediums be allowed to tell people they are NSAC certified mediums by, for example, displaying it on their business card or on the internet.

I was fascinated to discover years ago that testing the accuracy of mediums was being conducted at the University of Arizona under the direction of a professor there named Gary E. Schwartz. Among others, Prof. Schwartz has tested famous mediums such as John Edward of television fame from his show *Crossing Over*, and Allison Dubois, the woman that the TV series *Medium* was based on.

Professor Schwartz's technique is similar to that of the NSAC board in that both are focused on evidentiary information. In Schwartz's case he places the medium in one room and the sitter in a different location, so the medium doesn't even see the sitter. Then he asks the medium to do a reading. He takes notes of what the medium says that might be evidentiary. After the reading, Schwartz talks to the sitter and asks detail by detail if the information is accurate. For example, the medium may have given ten pieces of information from the spirit such as "a man," "had blonde hair as a child which turned brown later," "death by heart attack," "was a teacher by profession," "owned a Chevrolet Corvette," "listened to classical music," "lost his wife before he passed on," "asks for forgiveness for an argument he had with the sitter," etc. If the sitter recognizes nine out of the ten bits of information as things he believes to be accurate, then Schwartz would grade the reading as ninety percent confirmed by the sitter. John Edward received rankings like these when he was tested, some of the highest given. [23]

If you are willing to travel, there is a way you can find some very good mediums all in one place. Imagine that you could travel

---

[23] Gary E. Schwartz. *The Afterlife Experiments: Breakthrough Scientific Evidence of Life After Death.* New York: Atria Publishing. 2003.

to a small town where dozens of the residents are mediums. There is such a place. It's called Lily Dale, New York. It is a charming hamlet where many of the homes were built in the 1800s when Spiritualism was in its heyday. It hosts the headquarters for the NSAC. Only a few hundred people live at Lily Dale year-round, but during the summer over 20,000 people visit. They come to get readings from the many mediums, some of whom only visit during the summer season. They also attend workshops, speeches, and other programs related to spirit communication and personal spiritual growth and development.

Finally, the four mediums I have received personal readings from and/or worked with and can highly recommend are: Sherrie Dillard, Ann Gehman, Cinnamon Mancini, and Claire Daugherty. Here are four that I would be very excited to receive readings from in the future: Theresa Caputo, Chip Coffey, John Edward, and Rebecca Rosen. You can find most of these mediums by simply searching for their name on the Internet.

29 - Mental Mediumship and Physical Mediumship

The practice of mediumship can be divided into two broad categories, mental and physical. Most mediums practice mental mediumship. That means the communication between the spirit world and the earth plane is taking place inside their minds. *Clairvoyance, clairaudience,* and *clairsentience* are the main methods for mental mediumship. These are French words that mean "clear seeing," "clear hearing," and "clear feeling." Someone on the spirit side impresses information into the medium. In clairvoyance the medium sees images, symbols, and words in their mind's eye. In clairaudience the medium hears a voice speaking to them. Clairsentience is a little harder to describe; the medium "feels" the information within themselves. When I practice clairsentience, I feel like I have entered a different state of consciousness. I know this may sound strange, but I feel like in addition to my brain, the information is coming into my heart. I receive emotions as well as information. It is as if I am feeling what the spirit is feeling. Sometimes I begin to weep uncontrollably. When I attempt to verbalize what the spirit is channeling, I don't see it or hear it, I feel it. I have a strong sense of something I would call a "knowingness."

For example, somehow, I might know that in the past the spirit and the sitter had some strong argument over something, and that the spirit wants to ask the sitter for forgiveness. I don't know how I know; I just know. So, I will mention this information to the sitter, and if the sitter confirms it, it helps me continue deeper into the communication. It can be very emotional, and sometimes after readings like this I feel worn out, sensing the need to find a quiet place to recharge my batteries.

Physical mediumship is another category entirely. The simplest way to define it is to say that if something physically moves without a physical person touching it, that is physical mediumship.

When Modern Spiritualism was born in 1848, it was heralded by physical mediumship called the *Hydesville rappings*. Rapping is a phenomenon that takes place when a spirit knocks on a physical object such as a door, wall, or a table. Hydesville is a rural community about thirty miles east of Rochester in upstate New York. It had a small cottage inhabited by the Fox family who had moved there a few months before the birthday of Modern Spiritualism which took place there on the evening of March 31 of that year. Soon after they moved in, they were subject to *poltergeist* activity. A poltergeist is a spirit that causes physical phenomena such as rappings and the movement of objects.

Poltergeist activity has been around since prehistoric times, but the rappings that took place in the Hydesville cottage are unique because the Fox family developed a code by which the spirit was able to answer their questions. For example, they might ask the spirit "yes or no" questions and get one rap for "yes," and two raps for "no." An endless flow of information then began to flow from the spirit world to the physical world through this slow and primitive method of communication.

Examples of physical mediumship are endless. In the nineteenth century, *table tipping* was widely practiced. This was a type of seance where people would sit around a table, place their hands on it, and observe the table move, tilt, or rotate in response to their questions. Sometimes the table would even levitate, floating a few inches above the ground.

Another example is *automatic writing*. In automatic writing, the writing instrument, perhaps a pen or pencil, writes a message on its own while being held in the hand of the medium. Let me be clear. Even though the medium is holding the writing instrument, they are not moving it. The instrument is moving by itself, through spiritual influence. Even if the medium is not paying attention to it by, for example, speaking to someone while the writing is going on, the writing will continue of its own volition. It gets even more interesting in cases where after the phenomenon is completed, the medium looks down and sees that the message was written in a language that the medium doesn't speak or understand.

Levitation takes place when a physical object or person rises into the air. My favorite example of this phenomenon took place in England through the mediumship of perhaps the greatest medium of the nineteenth century, Daniel Dunglas Home. This is one of those examples when, discovering the account of this incident during my study of mediumship, I was left in stunned amazement. I have to take the incident seriously because it was performed in front of witnesses of very high British social status. They would not have testified to the veracity of this incident without being absolutely convinced; they would have not risked their reputations and social standing by doing so, something unthinkable in Victorian England. Here is the incident as told by the famous Sherlock Holmes author Sir Arthur Conan Doyle in his seminal book *The History of Spiritualism*:

In 1868 Lord Adare, Lord Lindsay, Captain Wynne, and Mr. Smith Barry saw Home levitate upon many occasions. A very minute account has been left by the first three witnesses of the occurrence of December 16 of this year, when at Ashley House, Home, in a state of trance, floated out of the bedroom and into the sitting room window, passing 70 feet above the street. After his arrival in the sitting room he went back into the bedroom with Lord Adare, and upon the latter remarking that he could not understand how Home could have fitted through the window which was only partially raised, "he told me to stand a little distance off. He then went through the open space head first quite rapidly, his body being nearly horizontal and apparently rigid. He came in again feet foremost." Such was the account given by Lords Adare and Lindsey...

Captain Wynne at once wrote corroborating the others and adding: "If you are not to believe the corroborated evidence of three unimpeached witnesses, there would be an end to all justice in courts of law."[24]

This was by no means the only time Home performed such a "miraculous" feat. I recommend his autobiography, *Incidents in my Life,* for those seeking more information.

---

[24] Arthur Conan Doyle. *The History of Spiritualism.* New York: George H. Doran Company. 1926. Vol 1. pp.196-197.

30 - My Experiences with Physical Mediumship

On a few occasions, I have experienced physical mediumship. The first episode that comes to mind took place on the second Christmas after Joshua passed on to the spirit world. Connie and I had received a message through spirit communication that Joshua would make his presence known on Christmas, and that we would know that it was him. After Joshua's passing, we gave away most of his belongings to friends and family, but one of the things we kept was a nice sound system that he had in his bedroom. It had an AM/FM radio, a multiple CD player, and some great-sounding speakers. Connie and I didn't have anything like that, so we installed it in our bedroom. Christmas morning came, and our family gathered as usual to open the presents stacked under the Christmas tree and have breakfast together. At some point I needed to use the restroom, so I bounded up the stairs for the *en suite* that was attached to our bedroom. As I passed in front of Joshua's sound system, to my surprise, it turned itself on. I stopped in my tracks and tried to see what was going on. The sound system had a little LED display in the front, that would tell you things like whether you are on radio or CD, or what track you were playing. The display lit up and said "Hello," which is probably what it always does, although I didn't pay much attention to it before. Being in a hurry to get to the bathroom, I just turned the machine off and went on my way. When I came out of the bathroom and passed in front of the music system, it turned itself on again. "Hello," said the little display. I just reached over and turned it off again, and it said, "Bye Bye." Again, this is probably what it always did, but I was starting to suspect that something out of the ordinary was going on. Finally, a few hours later on I went up to my bedroom for some reason, and the sound system turned itself on again. "Hello," it said again. And that's when it hit me.

"This is Josh," I thought. "It makes all the sense in the world. This was his sound system, so his energy is all over this thing. If he was determined to manipulate some electrical device in the house, this would be the one."

Can I prove it was Josh? No. But I would bet the deed to my house that it was. Think about it. This sound system never turned itself on accidentally before, then it does so three times on Christmas Day, fulfilling a prophetic message, and then it never does it again. Coincidence? I don't think so.

A second experience with physical mediumship also revolved around Joshua. I told this story earlier in my second book *Reconciled by the Light, Book II:*

> After I spoke and did platform readings at a Spiritual Frontiers Fellowship program, Connie and I conducted a workshop at my home for several people who wanted to know more about spirit communication, develop their own psychic abilities, and receive readings from me.
>
> The day before the workshop, we prepared the family room to receive the participants. It's a large room with a fireplace in the front, and over the

fireplace was a picture of the signing of the United States Constitution. It had been hanging there undisturbed for more than twenty years. On that day, when I looked at the picture, I was surprised to see that somehow the print had become separated from the matting and was hanging crooked inside the frame. It had been fine the day before.

"I wonder how that happened," I said to Connie. "No problem. I can probably fix that in no time."

I took the picture down, thinking I could pop the frame right open and reattach the print with a piece of Scotch tape, but then I saw that the backing had been thoroughly sealed on all four sides with heavy packaging tape.

"Man! We don't have time to fix this right now. I'm just going to put it in my office for later," I said, and carried the picture over to the adjoining room. "Do we have another picture we can hang there in its place?" I asked, looking around in my office.

"I don't know," said Connie.

"Oh well," I replied. "We'll think of something later."

The missing picture left a big empty space right in the center of the room, where everybody's eyes would be facing during the workshop.

"Boy, that sure doesn't look right," I thought.

In the afternoon I lay down to take a nap and while I was half-asleep Joshua appeared to me. He only showed me his face but, oddly enough, he showed it in profile. I didn't mind at all because I could see all the details of the side of his face: his cheek with the peach-fuzz on it, his ear, and the way his hair curled over it. I was so happy to see his beautiful face. Then he showed me his entire body. He was standing, facing the fireplace with his right arm extended, pointing at the empty space above the mantel where the picture had been. I didn't hear any words, but nevertheless I could sense that he wanted us to hang a picture of him in that space.

I got up, found Connie, and told her what had happened.

"What picture of Josh can we hang there?" I asked her.

"What about his high school portrait hanging in the dining room," she replied.

"I don't like that picture," I said. "His eyes look weird to me in that one."

There was a moment of silence as we racked our brains.

"Hey, wait a minute!" I exclaimed. "What about that other one in the bedroom?"

I sprinted up the stairs and grabbed a really beautiful photo that we had liked so much that we had it enlarged and framed. As I brought it down to show Connie, I noticed something that confirmed the spiritual vision of Joshua; the photo was of his face only, in profile.

I think that the reason Joshua wanted that photo hanging in the workshop space was that it created some type of connecting point or portal for him to more easily participate in the workshop . . . .

We held our first workshop the next day, and during the lunch break a few of the participants wandered outside on our back deck. Although I didn't know it at the time, one of the ladies who went out there was already a very gifted medium. She is a professional medium in the Raleigh, North Carolina area. When we gathered back to begin the second part of the workshop, Alma raised her hand.

"Yes," I said.

"I received a message during lunch, and I'm supposed to share it with the whole group," she said.

"Go right ahead," I said, intrigued.

"When I was out on the deck, Joshua came to me," Alma said. "He asked me 'Are you enjoying the workshop?' I said 'Yes.' Then he said, 'My dad's pretty awesome, isn't he?' and I said 'Yes.' So, he just wants everybody to know that he's very involved with what's going on here today."

That's the way it's been ever since. In every workshop we've had, at least one person has had a direct encounter with Joshua. [25]

Of course, this is a really fascinating story about how Josh continues to work with us from the spirit world. What I want to call attention to here is how this is also an example of physical mediumship. In order to get us to hang his portrait in the center of the workshop room, Josh had to solve the problem of the picture that was already hanging there. Again, I would bet the deed to my house that Josh was able to detach the painting from its matting, so I would have to take it down. Also, he must have known that it would have been impossible for me to fix it right away and hang it back up, creating the need for another picture in that spot. This whole incident still amazes me every time I think about it.

---

[25] Ron Pappalardo. *Reconciled by the Light Book II: Spirit Messages from a Teen Suicide: Adventures of a Psychic Medium.* Charleston, South Carolina: CreateSpace Books. 2013. pp.24-26.

31 - Spirits Who Materialize

There is a strange story in the Hebrew Bible from which we derive the idiom "the writing on the wall," a saying that means something bad is about to happen. What most people don't know is that the writing was done by a disembodied hand.

The story takes place in ancient Babylon, where the king is giving a banquet for a thousand prestigious guests. The hand materializes and writes a message on the wall predicting that the king's reign is coming to an end. That night he is assassinated.[26]

Another example of materialization involves Jesus. On the Sunday after he was crucified, he began appearing to some of his followers. On more than one occasion, the resurrected Jesus breaks bread and eats with them. He could appear suddenly out of nowhere, his form would feel solid to the touch, and he could disappear instantly. These appearances went on for forty days. In the last encounter, while Jesus gives them a final blessing, his form begins to levitate, rising into the air until it becomes obscured by a cloud and disappears.

---

[26] Dan. 5:1-30 (NRSV)

When I was a young man, I thought that there was no way these things could have happened as written. I thought that the writing on the wall was probably some person sticking their hand out from behind a curtain, so the rest of his body was hidden from view. The appearances of Jesus I had no explanation for, but I didn't believe these things could have happened either.

After Josh passed away, I began to study Modern Spiritualism. Once again, my belief system was challenged, and I had to reconsider these passages in a different light. Credible reports by distinguished British observers of the levitations of Daniel Dunglas Home and other similar incidents convinced me to accept that physical objects and persons have sometimes levitated.

The evidence compels me to accept *materialization* as well. Numerous reports of materializations began to appear shortly after the outbreak of Modern Spiritualism in 1848. At first, they consisted largely of disembodied hands. They progressed to include disembodied faces and heads, then entire upper bodies from the waist up, and finally complete bodies, called *full-body materializations*. I cannot deny the reality of this phenomenon because of some of the prestigious names associated with it. Sir William Crookes, President of the British Royal Society, the most distinguished body of scientists in Great Britain; French Professor Charles Richet, who won the Nobel Prize for his research on anaphylaxis; and Professor William J. Crawford of Queens University in Belfast, Ireland are just three of the many eminent scientists who observed and researched materialization phenomena. The research of Sir William Crookes in particular made a powerful impression on me not only because he meticulously reported the phenomena surrounding the medium Florence Cook, who repeatedly produced a materialized spirit who spoke and identified herself as Katie King, but also because he was able to produce photographs of the materialized spirit.[27]

I do not find the materialization phenomenon itself to be the most important issue. It is the implications behind it that I find most significant. If materializations are true, we have to accept that there is more to reality than what we can perceive with our five physical senses. We have to accept the existence of a spiritual dimension, that there are other realms that can move in and out of our dimension under certain circumstances. We also have to accept survivability as a reality. When, for example, through the materialization mediumship of the great Brazilian medium Carmine Mirabelli, the fourteen-year-old deceased daughter of a doctor who was present at one of his seances appeared as a full-body materialization, spoke to her father, and then physically embraced him, we have to conclude that this daughter still exists in a spiritual dimension even though her physical body has died.

Under the weight of this evidence, along with the immeasurable amount of evidence brought forth by other spiritual phenomena, the worldview of materialism collapses. This means that human beings are not just the random accident of a mindless evolution, but are immortal spiritual beings created by an unseen Intelligence and have profound meaning and purpose to their lives. This is a hopeful and inspiring discovery. It is my hope that this discovery will soon become obvious for all the people of the world to see. Perhaps the discoveries described in the next chapter will be the deciding catalyst.

---

[27] Sir Arthur Conan Doyle gives detailed accounts of the research of these and other scientists in his book *The History of Spiritualism*.

32 - The Future of Mediumship

Mediumship is a subject that has become more widely accepted in today's society. When I was first exposed to it in the 1970s, that was not the case. There was still quite a stigma attached to spirit communication, and most people were reluctant to talk about it. Many people did, and some still do, equate mediumship with witchcraft. That mindset has diminished considerably now that mediumship has entered the cultural mainstream. Numerous television shows and movies have been produced in recent years that have taken away a lot of the mystery, fear and stigma surrounding communication with spirits. The popularity of mediums such as John Edward, Theresa Caputo of "The Long Island Medium," and Allison Dubois has also gone a long way to dispel some of the negative bias previously associated with mediumship.

In addition, recent scientific discoveries are giving new credence to the concept of survivability after physical death and the existence of a spiritual world. There have even been advances in technology that provide hope that in the future the average person can own a device in their home that can provide two-way communication with entities in the spirit world.

The idea of creating some type of machine that could be used for spirit communication has been around since at least the time of Thomas Edison. He spoke publicly about his intention to invent such a device, generating widespread interest in the idea. Edison died before realizing his dream, but other researchers and scientists have continued the quest.

The Latvian psychologist Konstantin Raudive captured spirit voices through what has come to be called *Electronic Voice Phenomenon* (EVP), although the messages were very brief and sometimes difficult to discern. He published his findings in his book *Breakthrough: An Amazing Experiment in Electronic Communication with the Dead* in 1968.

About ten years later, clearer audio results began coming through *Spiricom*, a machine that was developed by George Meek and William O'Neill. It was two-way communication. You can listen to recordings of O'Neill talking to his spirit friend Dr. George Jeffries Mueller on the website worlditc.org at this url: http://worlditc.org/k_06_spiricom.htm They spoke to each other for a total of more than twenty hours. The activity has spread, and people are now communicating with spirit entities in various locations all over the world using EVP technology.

A more recent development based on research, initiated by Prof. Gary E. Schwartz, Director of the Laboratory for Advances in Consciousness and Health (LACH) at the University of Arizona, is called the *SoulPhone Project*. The SoulPhone Foundation website describes the R & D that should someday facilitate two-way communication with spirit entities. Their plan and hope are that other universities and institutions will duplicate their work. This is from their 2021 update:

"If independent labs at prestigious institutions replicate previous experiments, we can responsibly and accurately say that the question of afterlife survival has been affirmatively proven scientifically.

"This is a very important distinction to understand. Again, as of January 2021, it can reliably be said that life after death has been definitively demonstrated scientifically. If multicenter studies replicate existing data, it can be accurately stated that life after death has been proven. These precise statements reflect the degree of certainty based upon the collective research."

I'm very hopeful that this research will proceed to the point where it will be impossible to deny the reality of life after death—human survivability—and a spirit world. In my view, if successful, it will change the way we view reality to no less a degree than when Copernicus discovered that the earth revolved around the sun or Columbus demonstrated that the earth was not flat but round.

As the SoulPhone Foundation puts it:

"A paradigm shift will occur after worldwide announcements that afterlife has been scientifically proven. We are doing everything we can to make this shift as positive and comforting as possible." [28]

From my personal point of view, a wonderful thing will happen if this technology becomes as widespread as the cell phone; I will be able to retire from my profession as a medium. I imagine that mediumship itself will become a thing of the past, because communicating with spirits via electronic devices is much more

---

[28] Mark Pitstick. "2021 SoulPhone Project Update." https://www.thesoulphonefoundation.org/soulphone-update/ Web. 7 Jul. 2021.

accurate than mental mediumship. There is no need for the medium to struggle to translate the meaning of the images and symbols that come into their mind during a reading. Words transmitted through electronic devices are as clear as the normal spoken word.

Will I be disappointed to be "put out of business" so to speak? Absolutely not! If this vision becomes a reality, I will be dancing in the streets.

33 - Lessons I Have Learned

I mentioned in the introduction to this book that the journey I have taken since Josh took his life has led me to discard some of my old beliefs and embrace new ones. At the risk of upsetting readers who still embrace traditional religious concepts about life after death, I will summarize my findings here.

The first thing that comes to mind is that interacting with people in the spirit world has strengthened my suspicion that there is no such thing as eternal damnation. I'm willing to accept the idea that there may be places in the spirit world that could be called Hell, but they are more like Hells of our own creation. We aren't sent there by an angry God; we go there because we believe that we are not worthy to go to a better place. Like the Catholic monk I described who was afraid to ascend into the spirit world after he died, the guilt, shame, and remorse we feel for past "sins" convinces us—mistakenly—that we deserve to be punished. The reality is that eventually every "lost" soul chooses to ascend to a better place, even if it takes them 350 years or longer. When they do so, they will find all the help they need to come to terms with their past and find reconciliation, forgiveness, and peace.

A related point is that, in my view, institutional religion is doing a great disservice to humanity by continuing to promulgate the idea that God is an easily-angered judge or king who is quick to mete out punishment for the smallest offense. In my experience, God is more like a loving parent along the lines of the father depicted in Jesus' parable of *The Prodigal Son*. In that story, the son was convinced that because of his "sins" he was no longer worthy of his father's love. Only because of a famine in the land does the son return home in desperation, just hoping his father will hire him to perhaps feed his animals so he can have something to eat. He probably looked a lot like the *Aqualung* spirit I described earlier. To his utter shock and surprise, his father runs out of the house to kiss him and embrace him, has new clothes and sandals brought to him, and orders his servants to "kill the fatted calf" so they can celebrate his homecoming with a great feast. This is how anyone is greeted when they turn to their Father/Mother God for assistance, no matter what they have done in the past. It makes no logical sense to me that a loving God would be interested in consigning his/her children to something like an eternal Hell.

Many traditional religions have propagated the idea that God is exclusively masculine, but I'm aware of instances where God interacted with someone in a feminine form, embracing them like a mother embraces a child. I do not limit the Creator to manifest as only male; if anything, I would describe God as androgynous. I'm convinced that masculinity and femininity are both original characteristics of our Heavenly Parent, and God can express himself/herself in either form.

One of the most moving mystical experiences I have had took place when I was going through a time of discouragement. I had spent a great deal of time and money trying to find speaking engagements and initially had no bookings to show for it. Without my even asking for help, I unexpectedly saw into the spirit world and God appeared to me as a married couple. There were two

170

chairs in which sat a Father figure and a Mother figure. The Father remained silent, but the Mother spoke:

> "Ron, first I want you to know that even though you see two here, I am only one. I am only one. (I remember distinctly that she made an emphatic point of saying "I am only one" twice.) The reason I am manifesting to you as your Divine Mother is because it is most appropriate for me to come to you this way because of where you are right now in your spiritual growth."

Then she motioned for me to come over and sit on her lap. I took the form of a child and did so. She put her arms around me and held me with exquisite tenderness:

> "I want you to spend a lot of time right here during this period. I am healing you of certain wounds that you still possess from your childhood."

I wound up staying with her in this vision for hours that day. She just held me, caressed me, loved me unconditionally, and encouraged me. As I'm writing this, just being reminded of how loved I am by my Heavenly Parent, I'm choking up and my eyes are beginning to water.

Another new belief I have felt compelled to adopt is the idea that we create our own reality. Many people suffer unnecessarily because they attract it into their lives with their mental attitudes. If we invest our energy complaining, being angry, and seeing ourselves as victims, we are poisoning our mental and spiritual environment. I don't understand exactly how we do this, but I can't deny my own experience. Simply put, I know that I attract good things into my life when my mind and heart are in a good place, and I attract bad things into my life when my mind and heart are in a bad place. I make a conscious effort to live in gratitude, calmness, joy, patience, forgiveness, service to others, and humility. Don't get me wrong, I don't see myself as some kind of saintly person. I'm doing this because I perceive it to be in my best interest, just like everyone else does things because they think they will benefit by doing what they do. It's just that I have found that the kinder I am to others, the more good things come my way. In just the last few years, without me asking for it, people have freely given me new living room furniture, a car just when I needed it, money, lodging, home renovations and—above all—kindness, love, and friendship. I don't think these are coincidences.

I believe that the most powerful thing we do in our lives is think. A good way to train our minds to think good thoughts is by practicing some form of meditation. I meditate every day, because for me not doing so would be like not eating every day. It's good for me and it gives me energy—mental, spiritual, and physical. There are countless different forms of meditation. If you're not already meditating, I recommend trying a few different techniques until you find one that works for you. I have had good results using the *Transcendental Meditation* technique taught by Maharishi Mahesh Yogi.[29] I also had a great experience meditating with Baba Ram Das using the mantra *"Gate, Gate, Paragate, Parasamgate, Bodhi Swaha."* A very simple meditation that I do anytime when I want to refresh myself is to say, "God loves me, and I love God," as a mantra. When I breathe in, I say, "God loves me." When I breathe out, I say, "I love God." Even meditating for just five minutes will cause your breathing and heart rate to calm down, and if you have high blood pressure it can help reduce it. I've also used and am a big fan of Joe Dispenza's meditation techniques as described in his

[29]Jack Korem. *Transcendental Meditation: the Essential Teachings of Maharishi Mahesh Yogi.* Carlsbad, California: Hay House. 2012.

book *Breaking the Habit of Being Yourself.*[30] I think Joe's work is some of the most important being done on the earth today; he is constantly breaking new ground and may represent the future of humanity's spiritual development.

A form of psychotherapy that employs meditation at its center is *Mindfulness-Based Stress Reduction* (MBSR), a treatment developed by Prof. Jon Kabat-Zinn, who created the Stress Reduction Clinic and the Center for Mindfulness in Medicine, Health Care, and Society at the University of Massachusetts Medical School.[31] My son, Gabriel Pappalardo, PhD, has incorporated mindfulness meditation to create a therapeutic video game called *Amaru, the Self-Care Virtual Pet,*[32] to help people overcome stress, anxiety, and depression. The website *Headspace* [33] is also a valuable resource for this process.

One of the most important things I've learned is that what matters in life is not money, possessions, status, or prestige. What matters most is how much I have received love, and how much I have given love. Mastering the art of loving is the best preparation I can make for my inevitable transition from this physical plane into my next life in the spirit world.

I've also learned that one of the best ways to fight depression is to do something nice for somebody else. I had an experience in my twenties that convinced me that I would never have problems slipping into depression if I was serving someone else. It seems to work like magic every time I try it. It happened in Boulder, Colorado. I was living in a pyramid-shaped monastery across the street from the University of Colorado. Imagine about forty twenty-somethings living together like monks and nuns. Dating was not

---

[30] Joe Dispenza. *Breaking the Habit of Being Yourself: How to Lose Your Mind and Create a New One.* Carlsbad, California: Hay House. 2012.
[31] Jon Kabat-Zinn. *Full Catastrophe Living: Using the Wisdom of Your Body and Mind to Face Stress, Pain, and Illness.* New York: Random House. 1990.
[32] https://www.sixwingstudios.com/amaru
[33] https://www.headspace.com/

allowed, and everyone treated each other as a brother or sister. It was a beautiful experience.

One day, I fell into a strange mental state, feeling down, doubting my faith, and struggling with the idea of leaving the monastery. I retreated to the chapel, where I brought the matter to God in prayer. I prayed and prayed but found no relief. I told God I was going to stay in the chapel until I either dropped dead or this strange state of mind passed from me.

After a few hours in the chapel, I suddenly received a strong impulse to go downstairs to the large dining hall. Curious to know what would happen, I humbly obeyed the inspiration. When I arrived, I found a guest sitting alone at a table. I thought to myself, "This poor fellow, nobody's taking care of him."

I greeted the guest and offered to get him something to drink. Walking over to the kitchen, I made him a cup of tea, carefully adding the milk and sugar so it wouldn't spill. I returned to the guest, gently placed the cup and saucer on the table, and began to return to the kitchen. As I walked away from him, I stopped in midstride.

"Oh, my God," I thought. "The feeling's gone."

I came to the conclusion that because I had forgotten about myself and focused on the needs of someone else, the dark mental state lost its hold on me. I returned to the guest and listened to him pour out his heart, which was therapeutic not only for him, but for me as well. Afterwards, I was as good as new again.

34 - A Note to Survivors

A few years ago, a gentleman from New York contacted me after having read my first book, *Reconciled by the Light: The After-Death Letters from a Teen Suicide.* His son had taken his life by jumping off a bridge near their home. He was having a hard time getting the image out of his mind. He said it was like a video on a loop. He just imagined his son jumping off the bridge over and over again. I told him I thought that he needed to find a way to get this vision out of his mind. It wasn't good for him, and it wasn't good for his son.

Imagine if you had a son who wet his bed when he was a child. Then when he became an adult, you got into the habit of telling people about the incident. You talked about what a mess it was, and how you hated having to clean it up. How would your son feel about that? He would feel unloved and humiliated.

That's similar to how a suicide feels when we dwell on the details of how they took their life. I haven't communicated with a single suicide on the other side that didn't regret having ended their life that way. They are already full of shame and remorse for their action; reminding them of this painful episode by thinking about it over and over again is damaging to our mental health, and agonizing for the suicide.

I don't understand exactly how it works, but I have experienced that people on the other side somehow know when we are thinking about them. Especially if we had a strong emotional connection to them when they were on the earth, that connection continues into the next life.

In the first letter we received from Josh, he gave some excellent advice:

> *Please forgive me, and please choose a good experience we had together and record this as the memory you had of us together, not those last months and hours I had on the earth. This will free my heart and allow me to feel your mercy. I need that from you so much.*

The man from New York told me that his son loved to play baseball. I advised him to entertain memories of his son playing baseball in his mind. If I were him, I would prominently display any trophies that his son won and enlarge if necessary and frame any photos he had of his son in his baseball uniform. I would replace the bridge incident with baseball thoughts and memories.

There is a practice in psychotherapy that assists the brain in accomplishing this. It's called *Eye Movement Desensitization and Reprocessing* (EMDR). I participated in just one session with a local therapist and it changed my life. Connie was also helped by having sessions with an EMDR practitioner for several weeks. It's a practice that is recommended by The United States Department of Defense for treating soldiers who are suffering from *Post-Traumatic Stress Disorder*. It has also been helpful for people who are suffering from a wide variety of other issues. This therapy was discovered and developed by Francine Shapiro, PhD. She has written a pioneering book on the subject called *EMDR: The Breakthrough Therapy for Overcoming Anxiety, Stress, and Trauma.*

Another thing I did to help heal was to enlarge a favorite picture of Joshua and hang it in our dining room. Sometimes the picture seems to catch my attention. At times like that I will go up to the picture and kiss him on the cheek. I might talk to the picture by saying something like, "You're such a beautiful boy!" I'm convinced that this is beneficial for him in his new life; it's certainly beneficial for me.

As a family member or close acquaintance of a suicide, it is probably inevitable to struggle terribly with self-doubt and a profound sense of failure, "Why wasn't I able to protect them from this tragedy? Why didn't I do something differently? There must have been something more I could have done to prevent this!" Even if the loved one who passed on is not a suicide, it is understandable to feel this way.

As someone who has been through it, I would caution others not to dwell on these thoughts. Let them come into your consciousness and acknowledge them, observe them, and then let them go again like a leaf that slowly drifts by you in an autumn breeze. Let it go. Don't pick it up to get a closer look. Just let it go.

Recognize that there is a Higher Power present in your life, and let negative thoughts go by. If you dwell on them, they are very destructive. They can destroy your own sanity, your marriage, and your family. Cultivate humility, a humility that recognizes that you can't control everything. You do your best and leave the rest in the hands of God.

Also, cultivate forgiveness. If you feel that others have failed your loved one in some way that led to their death, it's all right to entertain that thought—it might even be true. You must nevertheless forgive them, and if you think that you have failed your loved one, you must forgive yourself as well. If you are having a hard time forgiving, ask for the ability to forgive, and you may receive it.

One thing that helps me forgive is thinking about someone who had a more difficult situation than me and yet found a way to forgive anyway. My role model is Jesus. I think about him hanging on the cross, his life slowly ebbing away from him as he bleeds from multiple wounds. He's having a hard time even breathing. He looks down at those who are executing him. In that tragic situation, an innocent man being killed in a brutal fashion, it would have been understandable if he had expressed bitterness, anger, or a desire for revenge. It never fails to move my heart when I consider that instead he raised his voice to Heaven and prayed for his tormentors, "Father forgive them; for they do not know what they are doing."[34] If he could forgive in such an extreme situation, I can forgive in mine.

Be honest about your feelings. It's okay to feel the way you do. They are valid feelings. Talk to someone about them, acknowledge them, but don't dwell on them. It's been my personal experience that if you focus on the needs of others around you, you won't fall into depression.

Humility, forgiveness, and honesty are powerful tools for you to use to get through the turmoil.

Finally, both Connie and I have found the old maxim to be true, "Time heals all wounds." Just after our loss the grief was so strong it could trigger and overpower us without warning at any moment. We might find ourselves weeping uncontrollably in a wave of pain. These incidents became fewer and fewer in the months ahead, and years later, I can honestly say that I am totally healed. A "silver lining" is that we have become much more compassionate towards others because of our experiences.

---

[34] Luke 23:34 (NRSV)

35 - My First Encounter with Spiritualists

Because Spiritualism played such a central role in my process of healing, as I bring this book to a close, I feel it is appropriate to share my first meeting with a Spiritualist community. This is an excerpt from my first book *Reconciled by the Light: The After-Death Letters from a Teen Suicide:*

> If you take the Green Line from Blackfriars Bridge heading westbound, the last stop on the London Underground is Wimbledon, the place of tennis fame. On Easter Sunday 2008, I made a pilgrimage there, but it had nothing to do with tennis.
>
> Exiting Wimbledon station on a cold March morning, I crossed the street and headed to my left. Dodging traffic and walking past the upscale shops, I turned a corner and found what I thought to be Hartfield Road, although the lack of a signpost kept me guessing for many steps, until I found one further down the street. The row houses here appear

to have been built in the 1930s, made of brick and crowned with the terra-cotta topped chimneys you find all over greater London.

About a fifth of a mile down the street on the right-hand side, there is a break in the seemingly endless wall of attached houses, and there stands a lone, small apartment building of perhaps four flats. Its plain, boxy architecture stands out in sharp contrast to the older houses on either side of it. The reason for the gap is sobering. This is where one of the thousands of bombs dropped on London by German planes fell during World War II, destroying the homes that once stood here. The apartments were built after the war in the space created by the bomb. The destination of my quest was not the apartment building, however.

Directly across the street on the left side of the road stands a small humble church wedged in between the row houses. Also built in the 1930s, this church at 136 Hartfield Road was partially destroyed during the Blitz, probably in the same raid that destroyed the houses across the street. Like innumerable places in London, it has been rebuilt and enlarged, to continue its unorthodox mission.

For, you see, this is no typical church. This is the home of the Wimbledon Spiritualist Church, a church that practices mediumship as a central part of its ministry.

Opening the door, I entered into a large foyer inhabited by a handful of people waiting for the service to start.

A young woman named Karen approached and greeted me.

"The service will be starting in about ten minutes," she said. "You can go on through the doors to the sanctuary if you like, or you're welcome to just wait here."

"I came all the way from the United States to attend your church," I said. "I've always wanted to visit a Spiritualist church, but there are none where I live."

"Really, how long are you in England for?" she asked.

"I'm here for just a few days with my wife. She's meeting some friends in the city right now. The trip is my gift to her for our twenty-fifth wedding anniversary. We're heading back home on Wednesday."

"How wonderful! Please make yourself at home," Karen said.

The walls of the foyer were covered with photographs. Some were large portraits of the church founder and other dignitaries. Others were simple snapshots of small groups of people posing together, the kind of photos you would expect from a wedding reception or even on the walls of a pub—people smiling and enjoying each other's company. I wandered over to a counter where I looked over some newsletters and other information pertaining to Spiritualism.

Seeing the young hostess was free, I walked over to talk to her some more.

"Karen," I asked, "how long have you been coming here?"

"About seven years, I think."

"What was it that brought you here?"

181

"Well, it was just after my mum died. I was having a rough go of it, and a friend told me about this place. When I attended the service, I was the first person the minister spoke to during clairvoyance. It was amazing! I've been coming here ever since."

"That's great," I said, "and I think you're doing a good job helping out here now."

I decided to go on into the sanctuary, and as I did so, I noticed a beautiful stained glass window of Jesus enshrined high upon the back wall. The light coming through the glass added a mystical quality to the scene. I took a seat in the third row and waited for the service to begin.

The congregation was small–less than twenty people.

The service was not unlike what you would find in a typical Protestant church: hymns accompanied by organ and piano, prayers, and a sermon. It was what happened after the sermon that was different.

"Now we will have clairvoyance," announced Karen, who was serving as master of ceremonies, from a podium on the right side of the altar area.

On the left, behind the main podium, sat a white-haired man wearing a clerical collar. He prayed or meditated for a couple of minutes, and then stood looking out over the congregation. Scanning back and forth across the pews a few times, his gaze finally settled on a man and woman sitting a couple of rows behind me.

"I'd like to address the couple sitting over here," he said, gesturing toward the couple. "Is that all right?"

"Yes," came the reply.

He concentrated for a few moments before speaking.

"I have here a gentleman." Then he paused again. Touching his chest, he spoke with confidence.

"I'm getting a feeling of tightness here," he said, "indicating this is someone who had a heart attack or maybe some lung problem like emphysema. Does that make sense to you?"

"Yes," said the man.

"He just wants you to know he's doing well now. The pain is completely gone, and you needn't worry about him anymore."

The minister moved on to a young man sitting behind me to my left, offering words of reassurance and encouragement.

"It's as if you've been going through a very difficult time recently. They want you to know that this period has now passed, and you are moving into a brighter phase of your life. Things are going to get much better now."

The young man appeared to be comforted by these words.

One-by-one, the minister went around the congregation. I'd say about half the group received a message from him, including me.

"They want you to know that for the last few months it's as if you've been a little withdrawn, kind of holding back," he said to me. "Now they're saying things are opening up for you. As if they're saying, 'Go for it!'"

This short message had a strong effect on me, and I noticed that I actually began acting with more confidence afterwards. In particular, I returned to the process of writing this book with a clearer mind, and a renewed determination to finish it quickly.

After the service, we retired to the foyer for tea and biscuits. I pulled up my chair to a table where the president of the church, the Reverend Ray Robinson, was sitting with his wife and a couple of other parishioners. Rev. Robinson was a large, good-natured man who in recent years had begun holding the mantle of leadership held by his father before him.

"I was elected, it wasn't an inheritance," he told me smiling. "How did you find us this morning?"

"I went on the internet. I was surprised to see that there must have been fifteen Spiritualist churches in greater London alone."

"It's interesting," Rev. Robinson said. "Spiritualism began in the United States in the 1840s with the Fox sisters, not in England. It spread to England from America. There are still many Spiritualist churches in America; I've visited several of them, although I must admit they can be hard to find sometimes."

"Yet it seems it has caught on more strongly here than in the U.S., doesn't it?" I asked and took a sip of my tea.

"Yes, that's true. I don't know why that is," he wondered aloud.

"I can see how Spiritualism can play an invaluable role in helping people heal from the pain caused by the loss of a loved one," I said.

"Well yes, exactly," he replied. "We're simply trying to help our fellow man recognize that there is survival—that is, that life goes on after physical death. That realization in itself is a great comfort to many people."

We talked a while longer, and the atmosphere felt as if I was among members of my own family, not strangers.

As I rose to depart, I mentioned again how happy I was to finally experience a Spiritualist church.

"There are no Spiritualist churches that I know of in the Raleigh area," I said, "yet, I am amazed at the number of people I run into in my community who are interested in things of a spiritual nature."

Then one of the ladies remarked, "You know, Ron, maybe you ought to put an ad in your local paper for all these people and just start one."

"You know, that's not a bad idea," I said, zipping up my jacket. "Who knows, maybe someday I will."

As I left the church and stepped into the cold London air, I could see my breath in front of me, and it felt as if it was going to snow.

I thought about what a coincidence it was that it was Easter Sunday, and that it had come so early this year. What was Easter if not the very day that Jesus demonstrated survivability, by appearing to his followers in spirit after his physical death?

Easter is associated with springtime and new life, with flowers and brightly colored eggs for the children. Yes, it was Easter. That seemed so appropriate, because after all that had happened since

Joshua's passing, I felt like I was the one who had finally risen from the dead.[35]

---

[35] Ron Pappalardo. *Reconciled by the Light: The After-Death Letters from a Teen Suicide.* 2010. pp. 100-104.

Acknowledgments

First of all, I am infinitely grateful to my wife Connie for her loving and unwavering support in bringing this book to life.

I'd also like to thank Dr. Adrian DeGroot for being the first person to read and edit the manuscript. His skills, insights, and suggestions resulted in numerous and essential improvements to the story. Professors Keisuke Noda and Charles Chesnavage offered crucial advice and supported me in its creation.

Dr. Sharon Lund and her staff at Sacred Life Publishers are wonderful people to know and work with. Ann Sandhorst has been a faithful supporter of our work for many years.

I would also like to thank the following people for their steadfast and generous support:

Maria Agres, Scott Avery, Susan Avery, Laurence Baer, RoseAnne Balogh, Barbara Bjorklund, Richie Clarke, Deanna Cooper, John David Doose, Burgi Ennis, Cindy Hamnett, Tyler Hendricks, Gene Huneycutt, Shirley Kanno, Jung Sun Joy Kessler, Rob Kitchens, Fred Lacroix, Jutta De Laet, Keith McCarthy, Joe Miller, Karen Mills, John Parker, Christine Proffitt, David Rueter, Sheri Rueter, John Pace, Shawna Pace, Klaus Schick, Kimberly Schlink, Michael Schlink, Charles D. Solomon, Louise Strait, Marilyn Valdes, Simon Voelker.

I also received support from the spirit world through guidance from my son, Joshua, and my other spirit guides.

Most of all, I'd like to thank my Heavenly Parent for creating me, being my friend, and sustaining me along my path in life.

In Memoriam

In memory of Donovan and Joshua Balogh, Kenneth and
Shiela Miller, and Brett Beingnesser, all of whom are cousins of
Joshua Pappalardo.

In memory of a beautiful soul, Crickett Lynn Allen.
Love, love, love.

In memory of Tom and Connie Sandhorst.

In memory of Jung Shim Rebecca Kessler.

Bibliography

Borgia, Anthony. *Life in the World Unseen*. Midway, Utah: M.A.P. Inc. 1993.

Burley, Philip. *Voices of Love from the Light*. Phoenix, Arizona: Mastery Press. 2018.

Choi, Charles Q. "Peace of Mind: Near-Death Experiences Now Found to Have Scientific Explanations." *Scientific American* 12 Sep. 2011. scientificamerican.com Web. 19 Jun. 2021.

Colburn Maynard, Nettie. *Was Abraham Lincoln a Spiritualist?* Philadelphia: Rufus C. Hartranft. 1891.

Conan Doyle, Arthur. *The History of Spiritualism*. New York: George H. Doran Company. 1926.

Dispenza, Joe. *Breaking the Habit of Being Yourself*. Carlsbad, California: Hay House. 2012

Frankl, Victor. *Man's search for meaning*. Boston: Beacon Press. 1959.

Goode, Caron B. *Kids Who See Ghosts: How to Guide Them Through Fear*. San Francisco: Weiser Books. 2010

Home, Daniel Dunglas. *Incidents in My Life* [Originally published in 1864]. Ithaca, New York. Cornell University Library. 2009

Kabat-Zinn, Jon. *Full Catastrophe Living: Using the Wisdom of Your Body and Mind to Face Stress, Pain, and Illness*. New York: Random House. 1990.

Kerr, Christopher. *Death Is But a Dream: Finding Hope and Meaning at Life's End*. New York: Avery. 2020

Korem, Jack. *Transcendental Meditation: the Essential Teachings of Maharishi Mahesh Yogi*. Carlsbad, California: Hay House. 2012.

Josephus, Flavius. *The Antiquities of the Jews*.

Macy, Mark H. *Miracles in the Storm*. New York: New American Library. 2001.

Mishnah, Taanit

Moody, Raymond. *Life after Life*. San Francisco: Harper Collins. 2001.

Pappalardo, Ron. *Reconciled by the Light: The After-death Letters from a Teen Suicide*. 2010.

Pappalardo, Ron. *Reconciled by the Light Book II: Spirit Messages from a Teen Suicide: Adventures of a Psychic Medium*. Charleston: CreateSpace books. 2013.

Puddicombe, Andy. *The Headspace Guide To Meditation And Mindfulness*. New York: Griffin. 2016.

Raudive, Konstantin. *Breakthrough - An Amazing Experiment in Electronic Communication with the Dead*. Lancer. 1971.

Shapiro, Francine. *EMDR: The Breakthrough Therapy for Overcoming Anxiety, Stress, and Trauma*. New York: Basic Books. 1997.

Schwartz, Gary E. *The Afterlife Experiments: Breakthrough Scientific Evidence of Life After Death*. New York: Atria Publishing. 2003.

The Holy Bible: New Revised Standard Version. Peabody, Massachusetts: Hendrickson. 2004.

Wickland, Carl A. *Thirty Years Among the Dead*. Van Nuys, California: Newcastle Publishing Company. 1974.

Young Starnes, Marion. *Letters from Summerland*. Cedar Mountain, North Carolina: Terra Nova Publishing. 1996.

About the Author

Ron Pappalardo

Ron Pappalardo was born in Los Angeles, California, to an Italian father and a mother of Irish descent. As a boy, he was motivated to serve God and know him more intimately. After nine years of traditional religious training in Roman Catholic schools, he left Catholicism to search for direct contact with the Divine.

After a series of spiritually transformative experiences, Ron describes himself as a mystic. He is convinced now that techniques such as meditation and something he calls "Journaling with God" can trigger a direct encounter with our Heavenly Parent. He conducts seminars and classes to facilitate such encounters.

Ron is the author of five books and is currently pursuing a doctoral degree in ministry. He lives in North Carolina with his artist wife, Connie, and enjoys spending time with his three surviving children.

Ron's website is RonPappalardo.com.

Other Books by Ron Pappalardo

Reconciled by the Light: The After-Death Letters from a Teen Suicide

Reconciled by the Light Book II: Spirit Messages from a Teen Suicide: Adventures of a Psychic Medium

Messages from God: 21st Century Prophets Speak for a New Age

Experiences with God: Stories about Mystics: A Guidebook to Your Own Divine Encounter

CPSIA information can be obtained
at www.ICGtesting.com
Printed in the USA
LVHW050008160723
752292LV00006B/474